Ashes to Beauty

A Spiritual Journey of Healing from Trauma and Addiction

Ashes to Beauty

A Spiritual Journey of Healing from Trauma and Addiction

Wendy Noll

Guardian BOOKS

Belleville, Ontario, Canada

Guardian
B O O K S

Dedication

I dedicate my memoir first to God,
who in His omnipotence has never left me
nor abandoned me; He has loved me unconditionally.

And second, I dedicate this to all
whose lives have been enslaved in the guise of
addiction, abuse, trauma, or the sex trade.
I pray you find freedom so in turn you can transmit
a message of hope, faith, and courage
to those still entrenched.

Contents

Acknowledgements

The passion for writing this memoir was birthed from a deep longing to leave a legacy for my children. I love you both from the bottom of my heart! My heart extends a depth of gratitude and love toward my husband, who has walked beside me through both the turbulent storms and joy-filled calms of life.

I want to thank my grandchildren for enriching my life with an abundance of joy and laughter.

I would also like to acknowledge my mentor, Michelle Sim, who encouraged and supported me throughout the writing process.

Foreword

It is an honour to be asked by Wendy to write a foreword to her book. This, of course, is a further reflection of the greater honour present in the doctor-patient relationship that we have cultivated; wherein the patient invites the physician, necessarily, to participate in their experience of their vulnerabilities and sufferings, to grow the requisite relational interactions and connections supportive of healing. The physician relationship is intrinsically, at its best, a sacred covenant, supportive of the movements directing us both toward our shared metamorphosis into health.

It may, in the outset, seem counterintuitive to say; nevertheless, healing is not a goal, purpose, or an endpoint in itself. We should not strive to heal or obtain a healing. Instead, we must all come to recognize, in time, that healing is a type of process—a way of being in being—entwined within the greater circularities of our growth and the broader movements of our human becoming. Healing is a dance we have been invited to participate in—will you accept?

In the beginning of our therapeutic work, we so often misguidedly look for a kind of magic to heal: a magic pill or therapy, a "right" answer; anything to fix the hurt or help make things "better." Magical thinking should never be confused with the true magic present in the wonderment of the world. There is no way to remove the need for our participation and effort. Life need be lived. In time, a patient may come to recognize that the world does not change despite our wishing and hoping that it might. In this moment, as a naive hope fades, a patient may find themselves changing from modes of childish magic-making to the perceived might of their moralizing.

Surely there is right and wrong in the world and, by extension, necessary justice, thereby making right all wrongs! For certain, many of my patients in the course of life have suffered terrible injustices in the form of non-condonable acts that they did not evoke and certainly never deserved. In the inevitable aftermath that follows, for a time, in the face of unfairness, they cling to the notion that once justice is served, healing will be the automatic consequence and natural outcome and they will be made whole.

So time passes, as it does, and maybe a justice is served, yet more often it is not, as those who harmed us are inevitably taken or move on from our lives, unrepentant and unremorseful, with no voicing of responsibility—yet the turbulence in their wake remains. The world we live in is not fair or equitable. My patients often bring a belief that justice brings closure. It does not, for closure belongs to the domain of our grieving. In this way, justice never equates with healing, for they are of different orders. Grief and healing dance in a way that justice and healing never can. Moreover, acts of justice are rarely in our control, or to the degree that they are, the cost proves too great. Ultimately, the unrepentant remain so until they do not. Certainly healing must not be contingent on that!

So we continue to stand, present in our wound. The magic of cure is illusory; a promise of a just world, even in part, has not made us feel any better. Then in this moment, not only in our loss, but within our loss of expectation, something truly and deeply magical begins to stir. It is in this moment that we truly start into and embrace movements that can be called healing. Now, I must tell you that I do not know what healing is. It is a mystery. I cannot dictate it. I am unable to control it. It defies my expectations of what I think it should be. Ultimately, it is a bestowal of grace.

That being said, as patient and doctor alike, we can tend to the conditions that are supportive of our healing and, together, recognize when it is present. Acceptance, surrender, the taking of personal responsibility, attending to the present, stepping outside of past wounds and future projected catastrophes, offering up gratitude, softening in our vulnerabilities, wisely utilizing the totality of our experience (dark and light alike), radical self-love and self-empathy—these are some of the perspectives we must shift if we are to tune or calibrate into our human becoming. Furthermore, we must discover that the labels of change are not what we seek in change. To talk about change is not to change. To change is to change. Change is holistic; our mind, our body, our spirit are not separate from each other, nor are they separate from the context of all of our relational life through time. In our healing, nothing short of authentic change will do—yet herein lies the paradox, as the change you can envision (i.e., wish for) is never the change you are being asked to participate in.

How then do we move forward? This leads us to a core dictum in our healing work; rather than know to act, we must act to know. If healing is to manifest, we must trade in our fear-based needs for stasis, knowledge, power, control, and pre-dictability, such that we may be open to learn through embracing a fluid and uncertain world, via our acts of curiosity, inquiry, play, and when necessary, our madness.

Magical thinking, justice, healing…where does this leave us? The answer is always surprising, for it is nowhere other than where we have always been! We have journeyed and travelled and fought and struggled and lost and fallen to come exactly to where we have always been. In other words, we find our way to the present moment, in all of its relational immenseness, lacking nothing, filled with gratitude, gazing at time's flow through wisdom's eyes.

Through the writing of this book, you will see Wendy's example to us all of "acting to know." Her telling her story and owning all of the feelings, wonderful and terrible alike therein, is her own therapeutic and healing act. Wendy's healing is for her alone (in relationship with the living world she is part of) to claim, and as a doctor, I have come to learn that it was never mine to offer. Moreover, in telling her story, Wendy invites us all into action, to tell our stories, but only in new and yet unimagined—and until stated, in unimaginable—ways. An old story told in an old way is a sure way to not change. An old story told in a brand new, inspired, and impro-visational spirit makes it a new story with each telling—all the while making room for new stories, potential and possible, that are waiting to be midwifed into the world.

In closing, let me offer a single suggestion to the reader: read this book with courage, as it required courage to write it. The feelings that will be evoked in the reading are your feel-ings and yours alone. When they come forth, do not run from them, do not hide from them, do not push them down or rain them out on those around you; instead, choose to turn your attention toward your discomfort, find the rhythm and flows they are offering up in your embodied experience, and begin to dance. In time, once the steps show themselves, you will look up and, with gleeful joy, you will see that others have joined you on the dance floor.

Dr. William Sutherland
September 1, 2019

Introduction

What does it mean to be in relationship—relationship with God, with nature, with others, with ourselves? Is it possible the deepest meaning of life is the journey and discovery of answers to these questions? Humans, though unique in form, are infinitely connected to all of life's energy. We each leave an imprint in the ocean of time that ripples to depths unknown.

We are born in darkness; a mystical journey that few embrace. Where did we come from? Why are we here? What lies beyond the mystery of death? Are these not the premises of all spiritual teachings? Our longing to belong is often guised in modern-day, temporal fixes that procure an aching for more. What if truth unveiled that our deepest longing is eternal; a longing that cannot be fulfilled in the dash of human life? What a freedom acceptance of such a possibility could birth!

A seed planted in fertile soil breeds a beautiful, fragrant flower. A seed tossed frivolously to rocky terrain has to fight to survive the mass of weeds and often withers and dies.

And for so many, the road to home embraces winding, narrow bends, hills, valleys, and darkened stretches where fear seems to encompass and grip the very core of their being.

My earliest memories depict a seed fighting to survive. Finding my way home has begun to unfold as my purpose in life. How does a child find the road to home if she feels trapped? If she feels frozen in the memories of being tossed to a barren and fearful land? How does she begin a journey when the beginning is unformed, a blank slate? A seed tossed abroad, trying desperately to find a safe place to take root. Trampled down, barely capable of weathering the storms alone. The flower—the child—becomes drained and succumbs to a blanket of winter snow, hoping desperately for rejuvenated life.

As a seedling's weathered journey unfolds, it develops a toughened exterior to shield the violent storms. Season after season presents a fight to survive, and in time, the beautiful fragrant flower withers from its original beauty and purpose.

A child, in adult form, desperately seeks to find her way home. She follows a map with no beginning. Gripped by a free-floating sensation, she feels lost and alone. Stripped of all distractions and means of escaping the pain, she turns and faces the darkness, determined to find her way. She wills to find her purpose in life despite the terror that looms in the dark.

Chapter 1

Rocky Foundations

That sinking feeling is back. Heaviness seems to hover above me like a black cloud. My body feels stuck in a constant state of fight or flight like an idling throttle awaiting a turbo charge in response to another flying obstacle destined for destruction.

Surrender is that sweet paradox lined with bitterness until it metabolizes the release of sweetness! The continual onslaught of painful daggers weakens my defense mechanisms. Where is my shield? It's there, but my weary arms can barely hold it in a defensive position. Alone in my head, a scary and lonely place. I'm longing for a reprieve, just a week or a month or even a year of tranquility. And what about joy? I reach for it and feel its embrace as it brushes by to comfort another. It eludes me.

What is this life for—I mean really for? Are we simply a grain of sand on a beach, a speck barely visible? Walked on, trampled, kicked, and tossed abroad with the ebb and flow of the ocean—to where, for what purpose? Do we resist or succumb to the status quo in the world? A broken society, lost and chaotic, is blinded by quick empty fixes devoid of meaning or substance.

How, oh God, to stay on Your path as the winds rage around me, swirling frantically from every direction? I long to be still, eluding the grips of this vortex, and find solace in Your beauty.

I see the gentle flow of embrace as I gaze at Your glistening river. I hear the sound of Your voice as You whisper through the willow tree. I experience the taste of Your love as a raindrop tickles my face. I feel the touch of Your warmth as the sun beats through the window. I smell the sweet aroma of Your love as I embrace the grip of my bike and ride free, surrounded by fragrant lilacs. My heartbeat slows, my whirlwind of thoughts downshifts, and my parasympathetic system kicks in. Ah, there You are, *Spiritus*, in the stillness of my breath.

After parking the car, I approached the emergency room and embraced the journey through the desolate corridor leading to her room. My thoughts ran rampant and were so familiar that I played them through my mind as though viewing a prerecorded movie. *Is this a false alarm, or will this be the last time I see her? How can I possibly share my heart with a woman who seems but a stranger to me? What was her life like? Does she really love me?* So many questions, but never the opportunity or courage to engage the quest for answers.

As I approached my mother's room, she lay lifeless and pale with her eyes closed. She had aged so much since I had last seen her. Something seemed different this time. There were so many things I ached to share with her, so many experiences I had yet to embrace. How is this fair, how have we lost what never began? So many nights I ached for her loving arms around me, for her nurturing and comfort. Just when I thought I could reach out and touch my heart's desire—a look, a word, a silence would rage at me like a razor's edge.

Snapped back to reality by her welcome hello, my heart jolted as I saw the pain and fear in her eyes. An unexpected urge rose within me, and uncontrollably I asked, "Mom, is Jesus your Lord and Saviour?"

As I held her hand, the room took on a bright yellow hue. Her face brightened with a vibrant sparkle radiating from her eyes. She replied, "Oh yes, dear, I would never have endured my suffering if I didn't have my Lord and Saviour! Oh sweetie, I am so sorry for being such a bitch. I love you so much." Our eyes locked, and we both wept years of tears.

The dam broke in my heart, and I felt a mother's love for the first time. The light in the room dimmed. She relaxed into the hospital bed, and the nurse came to take her to surgery. I stood captivated in the moment, afraid to move for fear I'd awaken from a dream.

⮜⮜⮜⭙⮞⮞⮞

A home should be birthed from an internal desire to create an external environment built on a solid foundation of nurturing, love, care, compassion, and safety. A child models cues from their environment, and their development reflects learned behaviours. As the child progresses through the stages of development, their behaviours are filtered through learned beliefs and values coupled with environmental, cultural, and societal factors.

When this does not occur and while weathering the storms of each passing season, children will desperately long to find a home safe enough to unveil their internal beauty and innocence. Lost and alone, they wander amidst the doom and destruction of a world gone mad, insanely chasing empty dreams and worshiping an endless need for more, to satisfy a void that can only be filled by love. Altruistic love does not know greed, selfishness, hate, lust, or darkness. Altruistic love knows only light.

❦

My memories prior to the age of eight are a blank slate, as though my origin was nonexistent. Occasionally, sporadic flashbacks would short-circuit my reality and I would question their authenticity. Like a child sorting through toys, I would savour memories of scenes in nature, animals, and acts of kindness from a neighbour. Unable to sort the taunting fragments of traumatic memories, I would suppress them to the dark crevices of my soul. Red rooms, two near-fatal car accidents, and a near drowning were unfathomable to comprehend as a child, so I would discard them as if disposing of an old toy.

My sister was born when I was five years old, and the photos from our childhood years enabled me to simulate a story that depicted a fantasy sibling relationship. Imaginary friends, creative fantasy, and dreams formed in dissociative states became a self-taught coping mechanism that would evolve into my adult years.

❦

"As a deer longs for streams of water, so I long for You, oh God" (Psalm 42:1). As deep calls unto deep—what is our deepest longing? Do we even know? As children, birthed in innocence, we long for a loving family that provides a safe, nurturing sense of belonging. As children, we long for a coddling environment that shelters us from the evils in the world. In a lost and broken world, the status quo forebodes a shattered reality of such ideals.

The awakening of my earliest memories is like a black rose gripping the internal red hues of my heart. A long country road that led to my childhood home was sparsely laden with houses and bloomed with an abundance of forestry, streams, and wildlife.

As an eight year old, I would often find solace with the animals in a small barn bordering the back of our property. I loved nature and the outdoors and frequently ventured off to a nearby creek. Minutes turned to hours as I sat by the edge of the water. Tantalized by the sound and beauty of running water, I would fantasize of far-off places and adventures I longed to embrace. It was by the creek that I recall my first sensation that some unknown, gentle, caring presence was watching over me. Later in life, I would come to understand this was the presence of God. I found comfort and peace by the water that would last well into my young adulthood. My time by the water became a cherished secret place.

My memories are quite fragmented from the ages of eight through twelve. Competitive figure skating consumed most of my visual recall.

Venturing into this part of my journey brings a great deal of anxiety; dissociative coping skills activate, and my mind feels empty. Pausing, I begin to pray, asking God for the words and insight for this portion of my story. My head aches, and I am aware of emotional pain as I awaken to the years of trauma I endured and the associated costs.

Thirteen years of age was a pinnacle point in my journey. My skating career had ended due to acquiring a smoking habit. I was raped. My best friend was abruptly taken from my life by children's services. Years of repeated childhood molestation finally ended. We moved to a new home in the city. And my mom became very ill and was hospitalized for several months. Dissociative behaviour was an innate coping mechanism I used in order to survive.

As I write, I feel deep emotional pain in the present moment and tears brim the surface of my eyes. I am staring out the window, and it is as though I am transported back to a hill in the country. Lying back in the soft grass, I feel comforted as the softness of nature embraces my being. I can hide safely here— no one will notice I am gone.

With the setting of the sun on any given day, I would experience a familiar turmoil in the pit of my stomach. It would soon be time to return home and to embrace the life of what I termed the *night child*. Unlike my vivid sensory experience of nature's vibrancies, my home's interior was a hazy blur.

The details of my bedroom served my memory with more clarity. I arranged my room so that my bed was positioned in the corner by the window.

When I was a child, this room brought many experiences with the *bogeymen*. I would crawl into bed in the fetal position and often sleep with my red Bible. I would check under my bed for the presence of the bogeymen, and when I would rise back up, there they were. They would stand about five feet from my bed and torment me. I only recall what one of the bogeymen looked like. It was about seven feet tall with its upper body resembling a dragon and its lower body like that of a kangaroo. Its eyes were red, and a light mist of steam would come out of its mouth.

I would be gripped with terror and paralysis and could not access my voice. Often times I would sneak past the bogeymen and run down the hall to sleep with my sister. If I could not get past the bogeymen, I would rock myself to sleep by embracing my red Bible and singing "Jesus Loves Me." My room during the day was always a safe place of refuge, but the night would bring much terror.

When I was a little girl, my sister and I attended Sunday school for a short stint. My mom wanted to equip us with a basic foundation of faith, but I found most of my spiritual ease in nature.

The next part of my journey is very difficult to articulate in words. I have spent a tremendous amount of time in therapy and healing ministries working on child molestation issues. I am okay speaking about them, but to actually write them down is a bit nerve wracking, to say the least.

A common occurrence in my life was molestation. Most of the experiences followed a familiar routine. I was sent to my abuser's location by means of a fairly common task request. I would routinely argue and fight—quietly screaming and hating adults for their insistence and lack of protection.

The steps to the *portal* seemed endless, and I lethargically approached my temporary destination. As I crossed the threshold to the event, there was always an eerie change in the atmosphere, met by an utterance of welcome.

At this point I would dissociate and find myself walking on a beautiful sandy beach with the warm ocean waves tickling my feet. The sun would beat down on my body and the wind would softly embrace every hair on my head. It was such a cunning trick. They thought they could kill my spirit and keep me caged in their sickness, but I escaped! Back in the room, the task at hand was ending and the ritual words would ring closure. This ritual of abuse would continue until I was fourteen years old, and then it just stopped. I have absolutely no idea when it started, only that it happened repeatedly for several years.

I recall one evening my abuser had been drinking and was fairly drunk. He wanted to speak with me, so I reluctantly met with him. I sat and listened. My abuser shared that he wanted to apologize for hurting me. I recall this being a traumatic reality to hear, especially since several adults denied the truth in this matter.

It was also during my thirteenth year that my mother took ill. She spent several months in the hospital to receive medical attention and healing for her illness. I remember the day that I was brought into a quiet room because my mother wanted to speak with me. She began to share that she wasn't confident in her recovery. She wanted me to know how much she loved me in case she died. She asked me to take care of my sister. I remember leaving that hospital room feeling like my whole world was destroyed. I felt disconnected and fragmented. I wept a flood of emotions for hours, and when the last tear dried up, I went numb.

❧ ⬥ ☙

Upon impact, an open wound oozes toxins as the pain and trauma gush out. Left alone, a scab forms and suppresses infection, which if left to fester could reach septic levels. Healing requires the application of nurturing and love. An acknowledgment of the injury, a gentle cleansing followed by a draping garment to protect the wound all help to soften the impact of trauma. If left unattended, the wound scabs over, locking the trauma deep within.

Around fourteen years old, I reached puberty and the childhood molestation suddenly stopped. I had my first drink of alcohol at thirteen years of age. My parents were having a large outdoor party, and some of the male guests decided it would be funny to offer me a drink. I can recall the sensation of rye as it flowed down my throat and into my stomach. I didn't care for the taste or the burning sensation, but I loved the way this substance numbed the pain. I had found my new best friend—a viable tool to help me act out the various roles that would protect me and would take control of my life. That night I also had my first experience with blackouts and alcohol poisoning. Everything I ate and drank made its way up, out and on the ground in front of the food table.

My mother did come home from the hospital, and I began my rebellion. I was done! I told my parents I wanted to go roller-skating with my friends and that I would sleep at my girl-friend's. I lied. I was off to my first real outdoor party. I drank, smoked pot, and experimented with a hit of acid.

About an hour after popping acid, a guy sat near me and eventually asked me to go for a walk with him. I was starting to feel the effects of the drugs and agreed to go. The walk is still pretty hazy, but I remember coming to a clearing with a large boulder-type rock. I remember being pushed and my head hitting the rock. I blacked out at this point but vaguely recall regaining consciousness twice.

The first time I regained consciousness, I saw him standing over me. He was pulling his pants up and had an evil smile on his face. The second time I regained consciousness, I heard my girlfriends calling my name but my body could not move, nor could my voice respond. When I was finally able to move, I staggered back to the party to discover most people had gone home. I managed to find one guy I knew and asked if he would give me a ride. He said, "Sure." I got into his car and thought I was going home.

Suddenly several men began rocking the car and screaming for him to unlock the doors. He ordered me out of the car, and I started to run. Catching me, they pushed me to the ground. They circled around me taunting, yelling, and laughing. They tore my shoes off and threw them into the bush, and then they started after my socks and shirt. I was wailing in tears of complete anguish. I was begging them to stop, and suddenly, by the grace of God, they did! I lay there in utter defeat. It seemed as though hours had passed before I crawled back to the guy's car. He agreed to drive me to my friend's but not before he made a detour and forced himself on me. Limp as a rag doll, I had no defense against any man.

I finally made it to my girlfriend's house and spent the rest of the evening in shock. Hallucinations and terror crept in concerning the reality of what had happened. I was a virgin before this horrible night!

The next morning I dragged myself home to tell my parents what had happened and met their painful words, "Well, if you hadn't have lied, none of this would have happened."

They shamefully took me to the doctor to have the invasive examination, which determined what I already knew. The doctor announced that I was no longer a virgin and there were definite indications of rape. I was given prescription medication to prevent the possibility of pregnancy and sexually transmitted diseases.

I also remember the rage and hurt my father had as his mouth foamed and he smashed his fists on either side of my chair and declared that I would "straighten out." My mother had just gotten out of the hospital, and my father loudly declared I would not "be the death of her!" My parents did not investigate the rape, nor did they press charges. Life went on. Another piece of me died and went numb that day.

The week following the rape was torturous at school. Numerous schoolmates, including the guy that raped me, circled around me in the schoolyard, yelling obscenities and spitting on me. The guy himself even approached me with that evil smile and called me a liar. I remember hearing the school bell ring and remaining in the field alone. I sat cross-legged and rocked back and forth with my hands over my face, cupping the pool of tears. No one came to comfort me, *no one*!

That would not be the last time I saw the man who had raped me. He approached me on the city bus a few years later like nothing had happened. I told him, with great authority, to never come near me again if he knew what was good for him! Not long after the rape, we sold the house in the country and moved to the city. This move caused more upheaval in my life.

It was shortly after I was raped and introduced to drugs that I began to change my views about men. I realized that I had something they wanted; therefore, I had leverage to attain what I wanted in life. I came to believe that love equals abuse, in all forms. If men wanted sexual relations with me, then I made a decision to give it to them, but on my terms! I vowed to be in control. I developed *roles* within myself. Dominatrix assumed the role of my protector and took control in the sexual department. I would dress, act, and role-play what men sought, all the while assuming full control. Dominatrix played quite the seducer, and in exchange, she was able to attain money, drugs, and possessions. She was wined and dined and treated like a princess. The illusion continued for years under the deception of a drug-induced state.

At sixteen years of age, I got my first job, at a burger joint. This job would continue to support my view of adult men as negative and unhealthy. My boss was a middle-aged man who entertained himself by flirting with the young teenage girls. He would often approach me, grab my bra strap, smile an evil smile, and walk away. It became quite apparent to me that grown men would exploit young girls through power, control, and manipulation.

I am experiencing a tight fluttering sensation in my abdomen area. My heartbeat is quickening, and I feel muscles tightening in my forehead. I am aware of anger surfacing as I think of the men who chose to exploit my body as if I were a defenseless rag doll. Was I walking around with "Abuse Me" tattooed on my forehead?

One of my foggy memories included my first suicide attempt, at the age of seventeen. I remember being found floating, face down, in a swimming pool. I vaguely remember partying at a friend's place and, in a drunken state, wanting to end my life. I regained consciousness in a hospital bed with my parents by my side. This was the first time I disclosed my child-hood molestation experience to my mother, and I remember her words so vividly: "You were always a child with a wild imagination." My rebellion and drug use greatly intensified after this incident.

<hr />

Sometime during my mid-teens, I was in a relationship with a twenty-six-year-old guy. His apartment was known as "the party hub," and he had an endless supply of drugs. This was when I was introduced to free-base cocaine. I absolutely loved the rush and can recall many weekends sitting around his kitchen table for hours free-basing coke, drinking, and smoking pot.

He lived across the street from a motorcycle clubhouse, and I could often be found sitting on the balcony looking into the yard of the clubhouse. I hungered for that life. I wanted the sense of protection and excitement that I observed there—a family, a sense of belonging. On one occasion, I left my boyfriend's house and headed across the street, only to be stopped by some of his friends. I recall being very angry that they interrupted my attempt to venture over to the clubhouse. They claimed I didn't know what I was doing, but I knew full well what I wanted. I had been in a clubhouse in another city a few times, and I had liked what I experienced.

Partying in the big leagues came with a price tag. I was involved in numerous drug deals and sexual exploitation. I was forced to watch men masturbate, which caused the internal, silent cries to rage once again. I had developed ways to cope with the discomfort in order to maintain the constant supply of free drugs.

As I stare out the window of the cottage retreat, I blank out. I have no thoughts, sounds, or visuals, just a familiar emptiness. The clarity of my surroundings is keen as I see every movement in the trees and in nature. The sounds are crisp and my breathing slow and steady. The flow of the leaves is almost hyp-notic. The wind gently caresses my face, and I am safe. I can always retreat to fantasy when I need to, even when in the midst of torture.

At seventeen, I met the first love of my life and decided to pursue a post-secondary education. I was accepted into a two-year business management program at a local college. I borrowed money from my grandmother to purchase a new car for school. I had worked in a restaurant the previous summer to pay for the college tuition, and my parents paid for my books and various start-up expenses.

My new boyfriend came from a family of wealth, and we would frequently hang out at his family's estate. I was in my glory: big-screen televisions, indoor swimming pools, a luxurious ranch with an abundance of toys and cars at my disposal.

I graduated from college and decided to put the pursuit of employment on hold because I was introduced to the world of crime and high-rolling drug circles. This decision resulted in laying aside all morals and values—this also involved not paying the debt to my grandmother, God rest her soul.

I can remember several times engaging in an endless supply of cocaine. Cocaine use opened the door to viewing pornography and engaging in sexual activities involving all night drug use. I vaguely recall occasions when I was drawn deep into the world of crime. I would go on runs blindfolded and carry the drugs. At the time I felt an unexplainable excitement and rush. I would stare down at an enormous rectangular piece of black hash with the gold seal still intact.

This relationship was my first introduction to physical violence. It was then that I learned to fight and realized that this guise of seduction comes with a price tag. I was willing to pay the price. After an evening of violence, I decided I had enough of this man's controlling, abusive behaviour and ended the relationship.

Shortly after ending my relationship, I met an attractive man at a party, and after an evening of intoxicated pleasures, I got in my car and headed for home. My seat was very wet, but I assumed that the rain must have seeped in the car window. Still slightly intoxicated, I began to drive. Not long down the road, my steering seemed off and by the time I got home, two of my tires were flat. I later learned that my ex-boyfriend seemed to have developed a fatal attraction and had been stalking me. He had located me that evening and urinated on my car seat and let the air out of my tires. Later in life, I had the opportunity to confront his behaviour and, through forgiveness, I was able to be at peace with the situation.

The road to home seems lonely and desolate as the roads of life twist and turn with the winds of change. Jolted off track by gaping potholes and blinded by raging storms, we aimlessly trudge our way through the wilderness. Enveloped by bitter heat and devoid of direction, we stumble around the maze with no oasis in sight.

At nineteen, I met a guy named Ed in a bar. I was attracted by the way he danced. I was looking for escape, a safe refuge from the memories and pain of my yesterdays. I began to date Ed, and around three months into this relationship we engaged in sex out of wedlock. I prayed to God for a child, someone I could love, who would love me unconditionally. My prayers became reality, and I was pregnant with my first child. For the first time in my life, I felt like I belonged, like my life finally had purpose.

During my prenatal tests, I learned I had contracted the herpes virus. Devastation and shame enveloped my being, and I shook with fear and disgust. Full of shame, I endured many tests prior to the delivery date. The doctors had to ensure the absence of lesions during the birthing process.

Shame encompasses me as I share about contracting herpes. I had no intention of sharing this experience until God showed me that the courage to unveil this truth could help others. I pray my sharing helps others obtain freedom from the shame and isolation associated with being diagnosed with an STD. To my knowledge, the only support groups for people diagnosed with STDs are specific to HIV/AIDS and hepatitis.

The pregnancy brought with it nine months of sobriety. Prior to the pregnancy, we partied relentlessly. Geographical cures (a term used by addicts to describe their belief that by changing their location their problems will magically solve themselves) started during this relationship with Ed, and we moved eleven times in one year. One move took us out west, which is where my beautiful baby girl was born. It was the decision to move out west that made me aware of how the influence of others distorted my ability to make decisions.

I met with my parents to share my excitement about the move out west. I experienced a ritualistic two-hour lecture, after which I was mentally exhausted and questioned everything I had ever done in life. I recall feeling depleted, useless, and defeated. I was discouraged and wondered if there was anything I could do right. In hindsight, I appreciate their attempt at concern.

Today I am aware that this lecture ritual began to embed a pattern of indecisiveness at a psychological level. Later in life,

I spent years in therapy attempting to integrate healthy, mature decision-making patterns.

I moved out west despite my family's efforts to discourage me from going. A lot of the trip west is foggy. I vaguely remember stopping one night to sleep. It was a 3000-mile journey, and we arrived within a week.

We stayed with my cousin Jenny and her family for a few days until we secured a furnished apartment, which ended up being a rat-infested dive. Not a pleasant experience when you are pregnant with your first child. We stayed there for a few months while finding employment and saving for our first home. We moved to a basement apartment and within a short time had it nicely decorated, including a nursery for the baby.

I pause from writing because I am experiencing a flashback—a violent incident with Ed that happened back in my hometown. Again my mind draws a blank as my body begins to feel numb. I am finding this book harder and harder to write.

As I venture deeper into the story, I recall healing in some of my relationships, especially with my mom. At times, I feel a sense of guilt and betrayal as I unfold the details of my haunting past. It is not my intention to hurt anyone but just to share my experience, with a prayer that others may experience hope and healing. I pray that my journey demonstrates that God restores, heals, and resurrects all that the enemy tries to kill, steal, and destroy.

I find it difficult to share the details of the next part of my story. I pause to take a deep breath.

Shortly after settling into our new apartment, I found work in a video store that paid minimum wage. I found refuge there.

On one occasion, I found a $100 bill. I asked a supervisor what to do about the find, and she said, "Finders-keepers!"

I am not sure why I am writing about this, but there must be some significance. God is clearly highlighting the contents of the book. Possibly the significance is to demonstrate how God provides.

I worked up until my pregnancy came to term. I made two girlfriends out west, who would later prove to be angels.

Ed continued to smoke pot during my pregnancy. He worked, ate dinner, watched television, and smoked pot. I was alone and isolated for most of my pregnancy. I went into labour two weeks early and was dropped off at the hospital alone.

I remember calling him at 5:00 p.m. to share that I was frightened, and he said, "Call me when you're in late-stage labour." I was so hurt and felt more alone than ever! I was miles away from my family and friends and ached for his support. The doctors decided to induce my labour, and I was placed in a delivery room overnight. The screams from the other women echoed down the hall, and I shivered inside.

Around 7:00 a.m., I was in increasing pain and went through one and a half tanks of laughing gas. At 7:30 a.m., they gave me an epidural and the nurse was angered to learn of Ed's negligence. She called him at home, and he arrived about five minutes prior to delivery. I remember screaming the word *shit* during one of my labour pains and the nurse scolded me. She insisting my baby did not need to hear me swear. I almost punched her out!

They wheeled me into the delivery room, and my beautiful baby girl was born five hours later. I recall her head was cone shaped and she had red spots all over her face and head.

I panicked, thinking there was something wrong with her, but the doctor assured me that was normal. I thanked God for this beautiful miracle. Within a day or so, I was to be released to the nightmare that lay ahead.

⁓⁓⁓

Ed came to take us home and upon arrival announced that he had lost his job. I cried so hard and wished I were closer to my family. I was so lonely. I longed for all of life's beauty for my special little girl. I wondered what this financial burden would mean for us.

I gathered up the pretty little plant that my mother had sent me while I was in the hospital and headed home. Upon arriving home, Ed bellowed, "What's for supper?" I was in a state of shock. This was *not* how I envisioned my homecoming after the birth of my first child. I attended to the task at hand and served up his plate of dinner.

Then it happened, the first of many violent incidents. I barely ducked in time to avoid his plate of food flying by my head and smashing to pieces as it connected with the wall with a loud crash. The baby woke, startled in fearful tears, and I wasn't long to follow suit. As I began cleaning up the mess through a pool of tears, he screamed the painful words, "Clean that up, you useless bitch, and next time I want you to serve up my food, I'll ask. How stupid do you have to be to let the water from the unstrained corn run into my other food?" I finished cleaning and ran to comfort my baby girl.

A few weeks after my daughter's birth, Ed announced that his three-year-old daughter from his first marriage was being flown out and that I was to watch her while he worked. I agreed due to fear and his routine guilt trips. This time he explained that his ex-wife was not able to care for his daughter.

Ed's abuse, through psychological and emotional tactics, continued to escalate. I gleaned support from two girlfriends. They took me under their wings and taught me aspects of child development and motherhood. I chose to nurse my daughter to try and save costs and create a natural bond between mother and child. The nurses had not, however, taught me how to latch on properly, and I was not able to continue nursing. My girlfriend taught me how to make formula and how to slowly wean my daughter off the breast.

When his older daughter arrived, Ed changed dramatically. His abuse got worse, and he constantly reminded me how stupid and incapable I was at being a good mother. If I were to talk back to him, it made matters worse. I had a flight booked home for a visit, and a week prior, his abuse exploded into a physical altercation that filled me with terror. The day after the altercation, I waited until he left for work and contacted my girlfriends. They came, with one of their husbands, helped me pack, and accompanied me to the airport. My mother had booked an emergency flight home for me. I was so frantic and fearful while packing. My friends instructed me to take only what was necessary. In a whirlwind of tears and panic, I left that basement apartment and everything I had worked hard for, including my car.

I recall that during the flight home, I looked down at my beautiful little girl and vowed to *never* let anyone hurt her and to love and protect her, no matter what.

Deep sigh and blank again. I feel that tears are there, but I am not able to cry. The truth is that I have cried myself dry about this experience.

My mom had arranged for airport transit to take us home. My mom's face upon arrival reflected shock and pain. She later shared that I looked like the walking dead and that it broke her heart to see me in that state. They embraced my daughter and settled me into the spare bedroom. Within a few months, my parents had my daughter and me set up in a beautiful new apartment.

My memories about locations, times and moves are somewhat foggy at this point so I will try to unravel the story further. God, please help me.

Not long after settling into my new apartment, I learned that I was two months pregnant. I was frightened and anxious about the news. I felt a great deal of pressure from others to abort this child. I was so torn. I could barely afford to support the infant that I had, and the thought of having another baby was overwhelming. I decided to go through with the abortion, and several days later the child was aborted.

I remember being in the pre-surgical room with my girl-friend and then being wheeled down on a stretcher to the waiting area. I felt alone and remorseful, wondering if I was doing the right thing. Looking back now, I realize that I had turned off a switch emotionally in this waiting area and wouldn't revisit the horrific situation until about ten years later. When I left the hospital, I chose to leave the memory there too. I froze the process deep within myself. I just couldn't deal with what I had chosen to do.

My daughter and I had been settled into our new apartment for a couple of months when I received news that Ed was back in town. I learned of rumours that he had been having an affair while he was residing out west. When that relationship failed, he sold everything, including my car, and flew back to town. We didn't officially reunite at this point.

Ed's first attempt to reconnect with me was while I was visiting my parents. He came to their house and was greeted by my father's wrath. My father insisted he leave the property and refrain from any further contact with our family. I was confident that my father would ensure Ed's detainment in prison if he ever got wind of this guy abusing me again.

<hr/>

It was while living in this apartment that I had an encounter with Larry, a man who would later become my first husband and the father of my son.

I met Larry at a party, and he called me a few days later. Later that same night, I heard someone outside my apartment screaming my name. Larry was walking toward my house from a nearby fast food restaurant, eating a take-out order. He was drunk! How attractive for a first encounter. This behaviour initially triggered a huge red flag, but in my lonely, wounded state I would ignore the warning. Larry insisted I come back with him in a cab to his friend's house. I didn't want to haul my daughter out at this time of night, but he was very persuasive. I entertained Larry's invitation briefly but then took a cab home. I couldn't tolerate his intoxication around my daughter.

<hr/>

After a brief stay at the apartment, I moved in with my girlfriend. I felt somewhat stable at her place until the parties started. It wasn't long before I was dabbling in cocaine again. On one occasion, while under the influence, I started to engage in a sexual encounter with a man and woman. I stopped myself before it escalated to anything serious but it was then that I realized I had thought of lesbian relationships and could very easily have moved in that direction.

During my stay at my girlfriend's house, I met an amazingly kind man named Karl. He treated my daughter and me like royalty. Karl was a sailor on a ship and worked long hours. When he was docked close to home, I would get rides to his ship and spend time with him. It wasn't long after meeting Karl that he asked me to move in with him; it was a fantasy that became reality. Karl wined and dined me. He bought me a car for Christmas so I could go see him when he docked and get around with the baby while he was gone.

During one of Karl's extended work trips at sea, I was homesick and planned a trip to visit my parents. While home, I ran into Ed and was drawn into his charm for an evening of disillusionment. I was full of shame upon returning home to Karl. I shared what had happened, and he begged me to stay. He passionately believed we could work it out. Karl shared that he was devastated because he was planning on asking for my hand in marriage. I couldn't accept that someone could treat me with genuine love and kindness. I broke his heart and moved back in with Ed.

I lived with Ed in a dumpy bachelor apartment for a few weeks until another abusive incident escalated. Fed up with his continued abusive behaviour, I moved with my daughter to a nice place in my hometown.

Blinded by wounded disillusion and numb to the core, I continued to sporadically date Ed. One evening during a lifeless sexual encounter, I heard my daughter crying. I got up to comfort her and the phone rang. I answered the phone to discover that Larry was calling. Drunk again, Larry was indicating he wanted to come over. I said no, explained this wasn't a good time, and hung up the phone.

Unfortunately, Ed had heard the conversation and became very aggressive. He gave me a head butt so hard I had a lump the size of a golf ball on my forehead. He did this while I was holding my daughter. I headed toward the stairs and he pushed me, causing me to fall down a very long flight of stairs with my child in my arms. To shelter her from the blow, I took the fall hard. Miraculously, I came out with a few cuts and bruises but was taken to hospital for a concussion to my head. The meds they gave me for the concussion caused nausea and vomiting. Ed stayed to care for my daughter until I was feeling better. Once I was on my feet again, I asked him to leave, this time for good.

———❦———

At this point in my life, I was overcome by self-loathing and depression. One afternoon, I attempted to take my life through an overdose of pills. While I lay on the kitchen floor feeling my life slipping away, I looked up to see my daughter staring at me. She said, "What are you doing, Mommy?" I began to panic and begged God to save me. I couldn't leave my baby girl in this world alone! I told her to get Mommy the phone. I called 911 and asked for help. My girlfriend came to stay with my daughter and they watched as the paramedics wheeled me out on a stretcher on route to the psychiatric ward. I spent a few days in the hospital and endured the gruelling experience of having my stomach pumped.

After being discharged from the hospital, I returned home to my daughter and tried to start my life over again. I was still partying pretty heavily, always being mindful of my daughter's well-being and safety to the best of my ability at that time.

It was at this time that I started my spiritual journey. I decided to attend the church beside my house. I went there a few times and enjoyed the experience until a man of the cloth made a pass at me, in my home, while bringing me a cheque from the church to help with Christmas expenses. This experience caused me to feel gut-wrenching nausea at the core of my being, and I did not step foot in a church again for years.

Engaging in a short-term relationship with my landlord's son caused another untimely move that led me to secure an apartment on the opposite end of town with a girlfriend.

Chapter 2

Reconstruction

The wilderness can be a desolate experience, with vast, empty terrain and no horizon in sight. Wandering aimlessly, we harden our hearts to escape the wretched pain. Pain, like that of a whirling dervish, rages at our innermost being and frantically causes internal chaos. Embracing numbness is similar to discovering an oasis in the desert, a tranquil place of rest for our weary soul.

My girlfriend and I secured an apartment on the south end of town. I felt a sense of emotional and physical security through sharing accommodations. I would soon come to learn that my girlfriend was related to Larry. Learning they were related created an incongruent internal state, consisting of both angst and excitement.

Enticed by Larry's good looks, charm, and status as a musician, I began to date him, and within three months, he moved in with my girlfriend and me. Shortly after he moved in, my girlfriend said she felt like a third wheel and moved out.

Within months, I experienced the first of many violent incidents. I foolishly ignored the onset of his violent behaviour. My ignorance would set the stage for several years of ongoing domestic abuse.

Shortly after settling into our new home, my daughter was scheduled for a visit with Ed. Bags in hand, she waited patiently, staring out the window, in joyful expectation of her father's arrival. She waited over an hour, silently anticipating a knock on the door. Suddenly she began to cry as the reality of abandonment set in. I would come to learn that Ed was in jail and his family had failed to notify me of his whereabouts.

Overcome with pain for my daughter's ongoing situation, I attempted to numb my feelings through the use of alcohol and drugs. One night, I attended a party with Larry and was determined to reach a state of oblivious intoxication. In a drunken state, I left the party on a mission to obtain revenge on Ed. This mission would result in my first brush with the law.

I had learned that Ed had been released from jail. Feeling courageous, due to intoxication, I drove to his house, intending to unload my anger. Upon arrival, I noticed his car in the driveway with the hood up. Ed's car was his prized possession. I walked toward his car and noticed his keys were in the ignition. My thoughts at the time were, *You hurt my daughter, so I will take your prized possession.*

I took his car for a joyride—sunroof open, tunes blaring. I was thoroughly enjoying the ride. Suddenly, the car began to smoke profusely and stopped running!

Feeling a sense of fear and panic, I left the car and began to run. I hitchhiked back to my car, which was parked in front of Ed's house. Upon arrival, I noticed a police car but, due to my intoxication, I choose to ignore the obvious and proceeded to get in my car. An officer approached me with an onslaught of questions and eventually placed me in the back of his police car. When the car door closed, my anger exploded. Due to my unwillingness to calm down, I was arrested and placed in handcuffs. After spending the night in the drunk-tank, I was charged and released to the street.

Arriving home with the rising of the sun, I was welcomed with fists of rage from Larry. His physical violence was coupled with verbal utterances of hate and profanity. Somehow I managed to lock my daughter and my two step-children in their bedroom. I gave them instructions to remain inside until I returned. Knowing the children were safe, I surrendered my body to the violent blows. I was unable to find the strength to fight back, so I resolved to a defensive position in an attempt to soften the impact. Larry's energy was finally expended, and I squeamishly found my way back to the kids' room. I quietly crawled into bed and lay frozen, trying to fight off the occasional whimper.

The domestic violence launched my experience of numbing to a whole new level. This incident was a pinnacle in our relationship—like that of a bull being released from its cage. The domestic violence escalated, as did my coping mechanisms through drug and alcohol use.

About a year into our relationship, I had became pregnant. This was a joyous occasion. The pregnancy proved to bring a welcomed reprieve from the physical abuse; however, the verbal and emotional abuse escalated.

The pregnancy was like an oasis in our relationship. We moved to a beautiful semi-detached home and created a warm and loving environment for our family, including a serene little nursery for the baby. I chose to dissociate from the memories of violence in order to feel a sense of renewed hope. Larry was aware of the isolation and heartache I experienced from Ed, concerning the birth of my daughter, so he made every attempt to create a pleasant experience for the birth of our son.

<hr />

I was two weeks overdue in my pregnancy. The decision was made by my doctor to perform a caesarean section because the baby was not in the birthing position. My surgery was a terrifying experience due to lack of pre-surgical instruction from the medical team. Unaware of what to expect, I was traumatized during surgery. While under anesthetic, I experienced anesthesia awareness, meaning I could recall my surroundings while under general anesthesia. Post surgery, I experienced an extreme fear of being buried alive. After our son was born, he was placed in an incubator and I was sent to the recovery ward.

Larry honoured his alleged love for me during my stay at the hospital. I was inundated with visitors and gifts. He spent hours hovering over our son's incubator. He catered to my son and me during our time of bonding.

Upon arriving home, my in-laws had been cleaning in preparation for our homecoming. *Could this be the dawn of a life I had dreamed of since childhood?*

<hr />

As I begin to write the next portion of my memoir, I hear an instrumental version of "Amazing Love" by Chris Tomlin. I pause to search Google for the lyrics. I ponder, "How can it be that my King would die for me?" I am in awe of the love I have come to experience from my Father in heaven. He loves me with an altruistic, unconditional love. A love that is inexpressible in words. I treasure His love and yearn for a deeper relationship with Him.

At the age of thirty, I felt a deep stirring in my spirit to confront my childhood abuser. I was on the verge of a nervous breakdown, and Larry insisted I seek counsel from a psychiatrist prior to confirming my decision. After disclosing a brief synopsis of my story, the psychiatrist discouraged me from confronting my abuser. She emphasized the likelihood that I would end up in a lockdown unit on the psychiatric ward if I followed through. I was confident that my desire to confront had originated as a nudge from God. I was confident that my motivation was based on hope that the truth would set me free and restore the broken relationships within my family.

Larry surrendered to my decision as long as I agreed to be accompanied by a family member. We set out on the trek to my abuser's house. I had forewarned my abuser about the purpose of our meeting. I walked into the living room and observed my abuser looking fearful and ashamed. His physical appearance resembled an aging old man.

My abuser began to share that he had told my family the truth and asked me what I wanted from him. I told him I wanted the truth and a restored relationship with my family. One of the members of my family uttered words that cut like a dagger to the depth of my heart: "Maybe you wanted it!" I could not believe what I heard, and apparently neither could my abuser because he firmly stated, "That's enough."

She was supposed to be my protector. How could an innocent young child *want* such betrayal from a trusted adult? I was aghast. I knew I was an outcast, but now I learned I was despised. Did she despise me or was it a projection of her own inner betrayal and self-loathing? In hindsight, I know that she was reacting from a place of deep-seated fear because I had learned the truth of her own dark secrets.

This adult was imprisoned by deep secrets. There was a generational history of trauma and sexual abuse, which aroused my curiosity concerning the possibility of similar abuse extended to this woman.

Unable to imagine what life must have been like for this woman, I somehow managed to extend compassion and forgiveness. Years of absolute loathing toward her melted like the morning dew dissipating in the heat of the rising sun because I had learned of her childhood trauma. I found peace toward this stranger—a stranger who, at last, I could forgive and embrace as a loving adult.

Life at home with Larry and the kids slowly settled into a comfortable routine, and with that came the awakening of old patterns of behaviour. I began to hear rumours of Larry having extramarital affairs, and his anger and abuse began to resurface. One night shortly after the birth of our son, my girlfriends invited me out. He agreed to watch the kids and had a few guys over to watch the hockey game.

My heart begins to beat rapidly and my face is hot and flushed. I pause my writing as if frozen in fear. Please, Holy Spirit, come and help me release this next portion of my story in written form. Grant me strength to face this horrific memory. Send your warring angels to stand guard around me—no backlash or retribution. God, please let these words offer comfort and encouragement to others. Let it be known that it is not my intention to hurt or cause harm to anyone mentioned in my memoir. My only intention is to help others and offer a means of inner healing to myself.

I initially resisted the invitation for a night out with my girlfriends. They persisted and insisted this was a normal celebratory event after the birth of a child. Although I don't remember much of the night out with the girls, my memories of the return home are quite vivid.

I was fairly drunk when I returned home. Larry's buddy was sitting at the kitchen table, and Larry was passed out on the couch in the living room. I sat at the kitchen table and had a beer with his friend. I begged his friend to stay the night because I felt terror as I envisioned Larry waking up in a fit of rage. He insisted that Larry had drunk enough to pass out for the entire evening. His friend left, and I made something to eat and retreated to the basement to watch television.

I heard Larry stirring. He then opened the door to the basement and called my name. He began uttering aggressive words, and in my drunken state of liquid courage, I uttered a firm response riddled with profanity.

I feel frozen, numb and unable to write. I breathe deeply as I try to press through the block that is hindering my recall of this horrific incident of domestic violence. I pray, asking the Holy Spirit to grant me the strength and courage to face the details of the incident one more time.

What happened next was an embitterment imposed on me from Larry that would ripple severe traumatic effects for years to come.

The door to the basement flew wide open with a loud crash, and in the blink of an eye, Larry bolted down the long flight of stairs. He approached me with great force and as he stood above me, his face resonated that of an enraged demon. Larry demanded I repeat what I had spoken and, in ignorance of the potential violence, I refused.

Then the unspeakable happened! With superhuman speed and strength, Larry grabbed me by the hair and began dragging me off the couch and over various pieces of furniture. The force of my body being dragged over furniture scattered lamps and various items. I heard the faint sound of shattered glass as a softened undertone compared to the raging bellows of his profanity. His verbal utterances spewed hate and rage.

My body began to ache, and I began to lose the physical strength required to defend myself. As the furniture scattered amongst the dishevelled room, I was finally dragged to an open space on the floor. Sensing the worst might be over, I allowed my body to relax slightly as I gasped for air.

Unexpectedly, the powerful force of his closed fist engaged my body. Full of rage, Larry punched my body repeatedly then began to use his fist to beat and disfigure my face. I managed to muster up what little strength I had left. I brought my arms up over my head in an attempt to soften the blows and protect my face from further damage. Through all the pain and chaos, I began to scream and begged him to stop. He continued his assault, and my body went limp and defenseless.

My only ability to cope was that of surrendering to the possibility that this may be the story of my death. I began to dissociate to my secret place.

Awakening from a blackout, I found myself in the fetal position on the floor, whimpering like a little child. I was unaware of when Larry had fled the room. Shaking violently, I became aware of the pain in my body and of the blood on my face. Paralyzed in fear, I remained frozen on the floor in the fetal position and eventually drifted off to sleep.

The morning sun crept through the window and radiated my limp, battered body. As I began to unfold myself, I found it difficult to be grateful I was alive. The physical pain was too great and the emotional pain even more unbearable. I managed to make my way upstairs to the bathroom. As I turned to face the mirror, my eyes embraced the battle wounds and I began to weep. I cupped my hands over my face as if preparing for a waterfall of tears. I somehow had to hide my deep feelings of shame and worthlessness.

What had my life become? Was I born to be beaten and abused by men? Was I that unworthy of love? As the powerful force of an ocean wave is tossed and beaten off a shoreline rock, there I stood, a lost, broken soul—heartbroken, physically beaten down, and numb to any concept of a loving, nurturing touch.

I headed to the kitchen to make a coffee and steady my nerves. In a few hours, the kids would be up and I would have to get ready for my daughter's birthday party—she was three years old today. *What will I tell the kids? How will I hide the wounds on my face? My eyes are so blackened and swollen, I doubt makeup will cover the mess.*

Larry appeared in the kitchen. Pouring himself a coffee, he joined me at the table. He was seemingly hung over and a bit dazed. His expression changed to that of horror as he noticed the condition of my face. He raised his voice, "Who did this to you? I will kill the bastard!"

In utter shock, I began to weep and said, "You did. You are the bastard that did this to me!" I immediately ran upstairs to the bathroom. Fumbling through my makeup bag I began to attempt to reconstruct my battered face. Following me upstairs, he slowly opened the bathroom door. He was full of shame and remorse. Hence, the vicious cycle of domestic violence continued.

Heading out the door, I grabbed my mirrored sunglasses to hide my blackened eyes. I needed to avoid any inquiries at my daughter's birthday party. Arriving at the restaurant, my mother-in-law inquired about the glasses by saying, "My son didn't hit you, did he?"

With a sarcastic undertone, I replied, "Oh no, I just ran into a door knob."

She said, "Oh that's good, thank God."

A while later, Larry's sister approached me with a demand to take the sunglasses off. After refusing several times, I finally succumbed to her request. Upon seeing the damage to my face, she said, "Did he do this? I am going to fucking kill him!" Knowing her brother's history with domestic violence, she knew he was responsible, despite my lack of response.

Utilizing my ability to mask my inner turmoil to the outer world, I survived the birthday party. I was able to divert attention away from me and toward my beautiful daughter.

Larry's sister showed up at our house after the party. She aggressively confronted her brother. She got in his face and made a promise that if he ever laid a hand on me again, she would kill him. He never physically assaulted me again, but the emotional and verbal abuse escalated.

Larry and I were married approximately three years after the birth of our son. The horrific incident of domestic violence drove him into a shame-induced state. He agreed to attend a twenty-eight-day treatment program. Faced with the ultimatum of "drugs or me," he vowed to achieve sobriety.

One night during Larry's stint at the inpatient treatment program, I found myself downing a forty-ounce bottle of vodka. I experienced another alcohol-induced blackout and alcohol poisoning. In a brief moment of sanity, I vaguely sensed I might have an adverse reaction to alcohol. I decided to abstain from alcohol in support of Larry's sobriety.

We managed to maintain a six-year term free from the consumption of alcohol but continued to dabble in various drugs. Larry's career as a promising musician led us to attend a litany of nightclubs. While entertaining in the clubs, we were often lavished with a free supply of dope.

Around this time, I had enrolled in hairdressing school to pursue a desire to become a licensed hairstylist. When I was a child, my mother used to have me style her hair and would encourage my skills by praising my creative talents.

During the first year of our sobriety, I was introduced to a twelve-step program. I felt out of place when attending the meetings because most of the members were a great deal older. During one of the meetings, a member provoked me to anger and I vowed never to return. Larry and I maintained six years of sobriety independent of a twelve-step program.

<hr />

I began frantically chasing quick fixes in a desperate attempt to fill an internal void and save my marriage. I opened a viable business in the beauty industry and bought a brand-new Ford F150 Anniversary Edition truck. Continued use of drugs coupled with emotional and verbal abuse eventually led to the demise of our marriage. We mutually agreed to a separation.

I secured an apartment for my children and me. I left Larry, began seeing another man, and started drinking alcohol again. Approximately a year into this relapse, I had lost my business due to blackout drinking and financial bankruptcy.

One evening, I went to Larry's house to drop the children off for their weekend visit. We talked about possible reconciliation. Our conversation ended in the usual bout of aggressive tones and verbal abuse.

Upon returning to my apartment, I had reached an emotional bottom, and in a state of hopelessness, I attempted to take my life. I downed a few stiff drinks of rum, lined a variety of pills in the formation of a cross, and had a knife on the table beside the pill cross. I called Larry to say "good night" to the children, but in a drunken state I slurred the words, "Good bye." My husband was familiar with my history of suicide attempts, and he came to my apartment with a few male friends. They kicked in my door, and we celebrated my failed suicide attempt with a table full of cocaine.

The following morning I drove myself to the local psych ward and surrendered my fate to the hands of their medical team. Family and Children's Services awarded my children to my husband. I lost my apartment. I was transported, in handcuffs, from the local psych ward to a nearby treatment facility. Upon arrival, I was taken to the lockdown unit, strip searched, and admitted to medical detox.

While in lockdown, I met a man who catapulted my recovery journey to new levels. He was exceptionally tall, with a bald head, dressed in orange scrubs. He was in lockdown for yet another suicide attempt. During this attempt, he built his own coffin and attempted to die by locking himself inside the coffin in minus-forty-degree weather. In the end, all he experienced was a bad case of frostbite and another trip to the psych ward—the fool.

Other patients in the lockdown unit had warned me of his violent nature, but I was fearless and unmoved by their warnings. During one of my mindless trips pacing around the circular medical unit, he said, "If you hold on for twenty-four hours, your experience on the other side of this unit will be like heaven on earth."

After twenty-four hours, I was stable enough to be transferred to the in-house psych unit for a psychiatric assessment. After the unit door locked behind me, I looked back to see him looking at me through the window. He had one hand raised up with his palm pressed against the glass and a tear falling down his cheek. I raised the palm of my hand and placed it on the glass adjacent his. No words were spoken, and I never saw him again, but I had an inner knowing that he was right—everything was going to be okay.

After several days in observation, it was decided that I could attend the addiction rehabilitation program. I completed the three-week intensive outpatient program in six weeks because apparently I was a "hard case." During my intensive outpatient program, I came into a state of complete surrender, which would set the stage for my journey in recovery.

Chapter 3

The Journey to Find Home

*J*ourney is defined as "the act of travelling from one place to another, of making one's way." When travelling abroad, one typically has a starting point and determines a destination. A journey toward *home* can become a brazen trek when the journey is riddled with twists and turns that darken the road ahead.

Embracing the edge of a cliff, I stand at a crossroad and drop to my knees. I cry out to God for direction. The road ahead is long and unknown. The journey has become tiresome and dreary. I am losing hope. One more step but to where?

Home is a place I have imagined in the deep crevices of my mind as a beautiful vivid picture kept safely hidden in a musical globe. As I awaken from my dissociative state, the globe shatters and reality shakes my being.

I head out on the journey to find home. I face a desolate land alone, praying for the secrets of my imagination to become reality.

Part of my discharge plan from rehab involved my return to the marital home. Family and Children's Services remained involved in our lives for three months, during which time I was required to adhere to random urine screening. I was also mandated to participate in parenting classes, individual counselling sessions, and relapse prevention and aftercare groups.

Losing custody of my children was the pivotal motivating factor that grounded my determination to maintain sobriety. I was adamant about attaining a way of life beyond my wildest dreams.

———

While in treatment, I learned that addiction was a progressive, chronic illness and that it develops rapidly in women. I learned that I have a disease. I ventured to grasp how to live a joy-filled life despite this disease!

The disease of addiction has ravished the lives of millions of people for decades. Many have endured its grip to the gates of insanity and death. Many medical professionals came to deem addicts, in the grips of their disease, as hopeless. Despite the staggering statistics to the contrary, I vowed to rise above the odds. I chose to become willing to go to any length to maintain sobriety and freedom. I admitted to my innermost self that I suffered from the disease of addiction. I accepted that without the birth of a new life, through a spiritual solution, I was doomed to a fateful, torturous, dope-sick death.

Willingness to go to any length to maintain sobriety was a simple concept, but it was not easy. Living life outside the security of treatment brought several challenges. I found myself experiencing many triggers in my environment and circumstances.

I began to implement strategies for healthy change in my life. I redecorated my house. I began an exercise routine and maintained a healthy diet. I disconnected from unhealthy people and made a painful decision to dissolve my marriage.

I returned home after treatment and I learned that Larry was still engaging in active addiction. I knew that if I stayed in the marriage, I would relapse. I knew that staying in a relationship with someone who was actively using drugs was not an option conducive to healthy recovery.

As I stare at the succession of words and gaze at the events listed on the outline for my book, I find myself entranced. So many memories to capture in these pages, yet I feel overwhelmed and confused. I am missing many fragments of my story due to trauma-induced memory loss and drug-induced blackouts. God, help me bring the fragments together to form some sort of structure to my story.

I also find myself distracted by the daily busyness of life and the societal vortex constantly nudging me to conform to worldly norms. God, please help me remain faithful and disciplined to Your plan for my life. Lord, draw close to me. Help me embrace writing as an oasis amidst worldly chaos, a place of respite in my healing journey.

During the early years of my recovery, I was plagued with bouts of depression. I recall waking up with the rising of the sun. I would pull the blinds down and roll myself into the fetal position in a desperate attempt to fall asleep. I would grip my head in an attempt to stop the negative, tormenting thoughts racing through my mind. If unsuccessful, I would reverse the ideology of cognitive behavioural therapy, meaning I would force myself to engage a behavioural change and pray my thoughts and feelings would follow suit.

Gripping the dead weight of each leg, I would swing them over the edge of the bed and slowly stand as I commanded my brain to engage my motor skills. The practice of healthy hygiene was not one of my finest attributes at this stage of my recovery. I scrounged through a heap of clothes on the floor to acquire my wardrobe for the day. I threw my hair up in a clip and raced out the door to get my children off to school and attend a twelve-step meeting.

After the meeting, I would walk downtown to a local cafe run by two recovered addicts. Because I was struggling to cope with a sober life, I remained at the cafe until my kids returned home from school. I tended to the norms of daily life at home by preparing meals, performing household chores, and caring for our children. Once the children were ready for bed, I dashed out the door and headed for an evening twelve-step meeting. This would become my daily routine for the first year of my recovery.

<hr />

After a year and a half clean and sober, I decided it was time for me to leave the marital home. I looked at a number of apartments and ended up securing the very first apartment I had viewed. My daughter and I moved to the new apartment.

I endured a heart-wrenching decision to leave my son with his father and stepbrother because my son wanted to stay with the boys. Two months later, I received a call from my son's school. I learned that he was voicing suicidal thoughts to his schoolmates. Utilizing the appropriate legal channels, my son came to reside with me. Larry and I arranged a visitation schedule for the children, which remained in effect until Larry's addiction spiralled out of control.

Larry lost the marital home through bankruptcy. My stepson suddenly returned to his hometown to live with his mother. Our black lab went missing in action, and Larry moved into a two-bedroom apartment with a fellow addict.

As Larry's addiction progressed, I did not deem it safe for the children to attend further visitation. He became vacant in their lives for most of their childhood years. I did not receive any child support despite court filings and legal enforcement attempts.

Determined to honour my vow to go to any length to maintain sobriety, I diligently accepted life on life's terms. My first challenge was to deal with an anonymous call to Family and Children's Services. Apparently someone deemed it inappropriate that my young children shared a bedroom.

Next I set out to find an economical car. I had diligently saved for a car while on a limited, fixed income. Having maintained over a year of sobriety I felt it necessary to pursue a career change. I enrolled in the Addiction Worker program at a local college and achieved my diploma, with honours, in a year's time.

Glancing out the window I embrace a meditative state in which my mind encompasses a mental type of rhythmic massage as I focus on the sporadic movement of the leaves. I feel mesmerized in a trance-like state and pause here awhile to enjoy the tranquility. My brain feels tired from constant memory recall, and I fight the onset of fatigue.

At this point in my recovery, I needed to enlarge my spiritual life. I had two girlfriends invite me to their church and came to learn they attended the same church! I began regular attendance at this church and found great solace and comfort in the weekly services. The church services were held in a local high school gymnasium. Most of the attendees dressed casually, primarily jeans and t-shirts. Tim Horton's coffee was permitted, the worship band was captivating, and the sermon style was intriguing. I looked forward to church each week and became active in their mercy ministry.

I attended numerous ministry classes and was water baptized twice. I participated in a healing ministry, which was geared to people who have experienced sexual abuse. The first year, I experienced God's healing power in the depth of my pain and one of the leaders became my spiritual mother. The second year, I quit the ministry halfway through due to experiencing a type of spiritual abuse that nearly landed me in the psych ward. Leadership dealt with the situation in a loving manner, but the experience traumatized me for several years and greatly hindered my spiritual growth.

The leadership changed twice, and they purchased a church building. With the purchase of the church property came increased spiritual warfare, and there was a significant change in the atmosphere. In my experience, I have come to notice that the investment in or purchase of property associated with ministry seems to shift the focus away from Jesus and toward the financial aspect of servicing debt and bills.

The twelve-step movement does not permit land or property ownership and has grown to help millions of suffering addicts for over eighty years. I believe it's possible that lack of ownership results in a humble attitude and aids in maintaining an altruistic focus in the hearts of people.

Several members began to leave the church, and after approximately nine years of attendance, I left too. My decision to leave the church caused me to experience a great deal of grief and turmoil. I had come to see many of the church members as family, and the latter experiences of spiritual distress triggered a bout of grief and loss reminiscent of childhood.

❧

Determined to capture a deep spiritual connection with God, I experimented with many spiritual practices. I attended a Buddhist temple and practiced prayer walks. I read several books on New Age religion, and I began researching Native spiritual teachings. Several acquaintances from church reprimanded me for engaging in occult practices; however, I chose to disregard their reprimand. I continued a personal spiritual journey in pursuit of truth.

Having attained a basic understanding of biblical teaching, I learned that Jesus hung out with prostitutes, murderers, and thieves. Jesus walked the streets, from city to city, sharing the gospel and the love of God with all who would listen.

God gave me an intuitive ability to see the hearts of people despite their choice in religious belief systems. From my perspective, people in the church acted as though I would catch a disease or experience a demonic infestation if I chose to hang out with people of different religions. I talked to God about it and felt at peace. God gave me an ability to learn from various spiritual teachings without the desire or need to adopt their beliefs as my own.

I acquired deep respect for the discipline of meditation from Buddhist teachings. I learned the importance of remaining in the present state from New Age religion. In my early thirties, I learned through genealogy that I have a Native background (Mohawk) and I became intrigued with Native culture. I attended Native drumming circles, learned the tradition of smudging, and developed a deep desire to learn more about the healing properties of plants and herbs. For as long as I can remember, I have been drawn to nature and continue to find spiritual grounding surrounded by God's magnificent creation.

~~~

Six months after securing an apartment, I met a man named Nick. He was also a recovered alcoholic. My girlfriend said her ex-husband, Nick, liked me and wanted me to cut his hair. Although she gave him my number, she was very bitter when we started dating. Nick and I connected and dated for a year prior to getting married. We had a small wedding at a local church.

My daughter has a beautiful voice, so we asked her to sing at our wedding. *I have often wondered why she wept through the entire song.* My daughter was also my maid of honour. She and my son will always be my greatest heart's treasure.

Nick was also a Christian. I believed that marrying a Christian would prove to be a promising endeavour. I distinctly recall my response to his marriage proposal. I stated that I still loved my first husband and that if he was ok with that, then my answer to his proposal was yes.

It has been several weeks since my last writing; I hit a wall when I started writing about Nick. It may seem vain and cold-hearted, but I came to realize this marriage was built on a personal need for security and the fear of being alone. Reflecting, I recall that since the age of thirteen I have bounced from one relationship to the next with barely a few days' lapse. Occasionally, I had the next prospect lined up prior to leaving. A six-month term of being alone seemed a huge feat for this girl!

As I embark on writing about my experience with my second husband, Nick, I feel my writing shifted to that of an intellectual documentation of events. I sought counsel regarding my internal struggle to write this part of my memoir. I was advised not to force any thoughts outside of those I felt led by God to write.

Nick and I moved to a beautiful main floor apartment of a house. I mention this house because I remember the tranquility of nature's embrace I found in the richly forested backyard setting. The yard's perimeter was lined with mature trees and a tall privacy fence. The yard was filled with bushes, rock gardens, a pond, and a beautiful flagstone patio nestled up against the house. It was a serene safe haven, like that of heaven on earth. I spent many hours in contemplative meditation embracing nature's sensory experience.

<hr/>

The serene energy found in this house was about to take a drastic shift. One fateful evening, my daughter was returning home from a party. I remember the tight, knotted sensation in my stomach as I looked through the kitchen window to witness my daughter being brought home by two teenage boys. There was one boy on either side of her to steady her as she walked. I would not come to know the horror she experienced that evening until years later, but deep in the pit of my stomach I intuitively knew. I sensed that familiar internal sensation.

My daughter seemed to experience a shift in innocence that evening, which launched her into experimentation with drugs and alcohol. One evening I received a call from her stepsister, who advised that I needed to get to the hospital immediately. My daughter had experienced a drug overdose.

As I arrived at the hospital, I held back the tears and somehow controlled the terror and fear. I needed to be strong and keep my emotions in check. Approaching her hospital bed, I noticed a conglomeration of machines and monitors. I witnessed nurses monitoring her vitals from a nearby nursing station. I bit my lip as I noticed her eyes rolling back in her head. The whites of her eyes were riddled with bloodshot veins. I stood by her bedside. She grabbed my hand and said, "Mommy, I'm scared." I felt my heart become overwhelmed with pain and fear.

Stuffing my emotions deep within, I scrambled to speak with nurses, doctors, and psychiatrists to establish a plan of care. After battling a great deal of red tape, I finally received the green light to have my daughter transferred to a lockdown unit at another local hospital.

Knowing that her plan of care was in process, I retreated to the chapel. I began to weep as I attempted to release the depths of heart-wrenching agony. Returning to her hospital room, the nurse handed me the phone. She stated, "Your sponsor is on the phone, and some guy is on the other side of the unit doors insistent on seeing you." Nick was unavailable because he was camping with his sons. God knew I needed support, so he sent loving friends from my recovery circle.

My daughter admitted to attempting to take her life. Feeling powerless to help on my own, I vowed to have her admitted to a youth program. The program would provide her with tools to learn how to deal with the pain associated from her recent traumatic experience. As the steel doors to the lockdown unit slammed shut behind me, I heard her screaming, "I hate you!" The shriek of her voice ripped at my heart and soul. I prayed for confirmation that I had made the right decision. I longed for peace in my soul. I needed to know that I had done everything possible to try to help her. My daughter was released from the two-week program and returned home with, from my perspective, a newfound hope for her future.

Shortly after these fateful events, Nick and I bought a house. We settled into our new house and life was fairly routine for about six years. We held stable jobs, attended church, and lived a normal life—whatever that is!

At some point during our marriage, my cousin Jenny returned from out west and begged me to get my motorcycle license. After a great deal of persuasion, I decided to overcome the fear and ventured to take the motorcycle course. I attained my license and bought a 750 Honda Nighthawk. Not long after, I upgraded to my first Harley Davidson motorcycle—an 883 Sportster.

I became passionate about riding. It was a freedom unlike anything I'd experienced. Riding the open roads was euphoric. I felt so close to nature and God. As I rode, the wind embraced my body as though the hand of God had touched me. The smell of lilacs tickled my olfactory senses. The birds flew around me, unified in a rhythmic dance. The shifting temperature currents tantalized my soul.

Nick and I joined a Christian motorcycle club and attempted to launch a chapter in Canada. We participated in several club events throughout the United States. On one road trip, we encountered a level-four hurricane—riding through that was a trip!

Not surprisingly, the Canadian chapter began to experience a great deal of strife and the chapter folded. The enemy comes to kill, steal, and destroy. In our frailty, we often succumb to the enemy's tactics to divide and conquer. I experienced my ego resurfacing when faced with a male-dominant ministry. I judged Nick as being a wannabe biker and was unwilling to submit to him because I knew more about the bike world than he did.

About six years into our marriage, we began to experience a great deal of strife. We decided to invite a priest and a few church members to pray through our home. I had often sensed an unsettling presence in the house and thought perhaps it may be impacting the slow demise of our marriage.

The invitation to pray through our home brought with it several peculiar experiences. They began by anointing our windows with oil and praying through the house. I was then asked if I would stand in our bedroom closet and see if a person's name came to my mind. Hesitantly, I followed the request and a female name came to mind. A box of old encyclopedias was found in the attic. A letter written on very old paper fell out of one of the books. The letter was addressed to the same female name that had come to my mind!

As people continued praying through the house, they reported having visions of seeing past sexual and physical abuse occurring in the house. One of their visions included a baby stroller being pushed down the basement stairs. I was then asked to sit on the attic floor, with the door closed, and talk to *ghosts*. Hesitantly, I agreed, provided the door remained open.

At that time, I felt like a spiritual child, so I succumbed to their ritualistic-type requests. As the day's events came to an end, I found myself in a state of terror and refused to sleep in the house. I spent the night at a friend's house. Fearing I would never be able to return home, I called a trusted man of God who met me at the house. Together we walked through each room in the house as he prayed quiet, simple prayers. I was able to return home, but our marriage continued to experience strife.

⬦⬦⬦

Nick left his job of over twenty-five years to pursue self-employment in the roofing industry. The business was taking off but suddenly came to an end when he fell off a roof and shattered his calcaneus. After surgery, he was prescribed pain medication, at which point, I became aware of his past addiction to opiates.

Nick began abusing his prescription medication, meaning he consumed more than his prescribed dosage. Escalated arguments became our norm. He agreed to go to a men's retreat to receive prayer and healing. Upon returning home from the men's retreat, I learned he had an undisclosed addiction to porn. A speaker at the retreat apparently triggered his addiction to porn. Upon learning about his hidden addictions, I experienced a great deal of anger. The correlation was glaringly reminiscent of the pain experienced in my first marriage.

⬦⬦⬦

Prior to Nick's accident, I had returned to work as an outreach worker. This job afforded me the opportunity to utilize my skills and education as an addiction counsellor. During this job term, I had two traumatic experiences that led to a medical leave of absence. The first incident involved what I perceived to be a spiritual persecution.

While attending a conference outside of work hours, a co-worker presented me with a question that caught me off guard. He said, "What does your Bible say about homosexuality?" I immediately felt a sharp pain in my stomach and heard a still, small internal voice say, *This doesn't feel right. Don't answer him.* I felt torn between avoiding the question to save face and answering his question honestly by explaining what the Bible says about homosexuality, so I answered. I felt hurt and betrayed upon learning he had taken offense. A heated discussion evolved after being accused of discrimination. Feeling wrongly accused, I disclosed my past encounters with same-sex relations during my active addiction and noted I had several homosexual friends, whom I love. Our discussion ended, and he seemed to be at peace.

Upon returning to work, my supervisor instructed me to contact my union rep and meet her in the boardroom. It was brought to my attention that my co-worker had filed a discrimination charge. If I wanted to keep my job, I needed to apologize to him in person, bring him flowers, and refrain from attending the agency he worked for. In order to keep my job, I agreed to the terms and sought counselling.

The second traumatic incident involved being trapped in an individual's apartment. I had safely secured a woman in a local shelter. Returning to work the following week, I was asked to accompany her while she obtained a few personal belongings from her apartment. Familiar with her social history, I deemed it appropriate to proactively alert my supervisor and shelter staff of our return to her home.

We arrived at her apartment and locked the door behind us. As she was gathering her belongings, there was a knock at the door. Frozen in fear, I instructed her to be quiet. The person on the other side of the door proceeded to urinate under her apartment door and rustle a plastic bag. I had a Velcro cellphone case, which forced me to devise a plan to *quietly* access my phone and call for help.

Overwhelmed by fear, I saw my life flash before me. I heard thoughts racing through my mind: *I am not going out like this. I am going home to my kids.* After what seemed like forever, I devised a plan to muffle the sound of the phone case in a nearby closet. I called the shelter to request police assistance. Some time later, the police notified me that the building was secure and it was safe to come down to the lobby. I brought the individual safely down to the lobby. We wrote a report for the police. She was brought back to the shelter, and I went for coffee with a co-worker to debrief. My shift was cancelled that night and I took a medical leave as recommended by my doctor.

❦

For the next two years, I sought support in the form of counselling and various church groups. I also maintained a holistic lifestyle involving an active exercise regimen, a nutritional diet, regular discipline in prayer and meditation, and frequent time spent in nature.

Nick and I accepted a leadership position running a coffee house ministry at our church. The purpose of the coffee house was to bridge the gap. It was intended to attract people who felt a spiritual longing but refrained from church attendance because of prior wounding in church settings.

One night while running the coffee house ministry, we learned that our evening speaker had cancelled. I scrambled to find alternative resources. I arranged for my stepson to lead worship, and I agreed to share my testimony. As fate would have it, God orchestrated an employee from a television ministry to attend the coffee house. After the event, he asked me to share my testimony on national television. In 2007 and again in 2010, I appeared on television to present my testimony to the nations.

Near the end of a two-year medical leave, Nick and I were in desperate need of financial provision, so I began an active job search in the field of addiction. The job search brought a great deal of discouragement. The credentials required for work in the field had changed. Professional and lived experience was underrated in comparison to university degrees. I am a strong advocate of education; however, I was not in a financial position to return to school at that time.

Setting aside pride, I accepted two temporary jobs: cleaning houses and working at a pizza joint. God began to teach me a great deal about deflation of ego and humility. God also shifted and disabled my poverty mindset.

As I began cleaning homes that belonged to wealthy people, I felt resentful and angry. Observing an abundance of children's toys and exquisite belongings fuelled my anger. I frequently ranted to God about the multitudes of children living in poverty and questioned the reasons why blessings weren't more evenly distributed!

As I scrubbed the anger out of my body, I began to hear the voice of God's comfort and gentle conviction. He taught me that harbouring bitter resentments had hindered me from embracing the riches of His abundance and provision. My heart was hardened, and I could not see my worth because I was blinded by hostility. Slowly, God began to dissolve the hurt and unveil His abundant blessings. I experienced a profound shift in my worldview and began to pray for the people residing in the homes we cleaned.

Shortly after recognizing these lessons in the house-cleaning job, I was led to another short-term position at a pizza parlour. The stint at the pizza joint brought about a lesson in humility. I observed my coworkers demonstrating great pride in preparing pizzas despite earning minimum wage. Learning to be content involved the practice of gratitude. Gratitude opened the door to abundance and blessing.

As the job at the pizza parlour came to an end, I decided to return to the beauty industry. Acceptance in the field allowed me to settle into a hairstyling position with gratitude. I quickly recognized a double blessing. Clients disclosed numerous heartfelt stories about family members who struggled with addiction-related issues. I was given the opportunity to enhance both their physical and emotional wellbeing. I felt honoured to offer support, encouragement, and attentive listening. When I surrendered and accepted God's will for my job situation, He began to redirect and reveal His plans for the next ten years of my life!

God's ways are not our ways. He knows the plans He has for us. Six months after settling into my role as a hairstylist, God called me into a new career—a career that would rocket me into the fourth dimension!

I was enjoying a day off when I felt a still small internal voice nudge me to check the job bank. Doubtful that I was hearing the voice of God, I resisted. I thought, *I am happy and content with my current employment. I don't need another job.*

I know God is speaking to me when I repeatedly hear internal thoughts that maintain a consistent statement coupled with a *spiritual knowing*.

I headed upstairs to my office, logged into my computer, and began to browse the job postings. Not long into my search, I came across a college instructor position for an addiction worker program. As I read the details of the job description, I felt a spring of internal joy and curiosity begin to bubble up from the depth of my soul.

An internal dialogue hosted by a critical voice quickly followed the surge of joy. *Why are you looking at that job? You don't know anything about teaching at a college level. You aren't qualified for that position. You don't even have the required academic credentials. Don't even bother wasting your time submitting a resume, it will only be discarded.* Pausing before shutting down my computer, I heard a conflicting thought, *Just apply—what do you have to lose?* I immediately turned on my worship music in a desperate attempt to drown out the onslaught of critical thoughts and submitted my resume online. Within a week's time, I was called for an interview.

> *As I pause to reread the paragraph above, I recall many bouts of the negative internal dialogue while writing this book. "Why are you writing a book? No one wants to hear your stupid memoir. You don't know how to write a book. You will go in debt if you try to publish it because you won't sell many copies. Do you really want the whole world knowing all of your hidden secrets?"*
>
> *Taking a deep sigh, I say a quiet prayer for God to remove these negative thoughts and give me the courage and strength to carry on. I feel an inner surge of strength as I embrace a deeply rooted belief that God will do for me what I cannot do for myself.*

A combination of anxiety and excitement permeated my being as I set out for the hour trek to my interview destination. Thoughts of anticipation and curiosity raced through my mind. Knowing I had a long drive ahead, I cranked up my worship music, trying hard to surrender the outcome to God. As I approached the college, I felt my heart begin to race and noticed my breathing was rapid.

I was invited into the office of the campus director and asked if I would like a drink of water. Half an hour into the interview, I felt a sense of ease and comfort as the dyadic conversation flowed rhythmically. Nearing the end of the interview, I learned that the campus director was a believer. The entire room suddenly took on a vibrant yellow glowing hue! Within a week's time I received confirmation that the college wanted to offer me the position. In that moment, God demonstrated that He could make a way even when a situation seems impossible.

There is a quote by Monty Roberts that states, "There is no such thing as teaching—only learning." It is a privilege and an honour to learn and to be gifted with the ability to teach others. This concept greatly resonated with me through my career in teaching.

No amount of compensation could compare to the depth of lessons gifted to me from my students. My students became a type of pseudo family. We shared experiential learning together.

Two significant events occurred during the first two years of my teaching career. The first event could be described as a *spiritual awe moment*. One of my students had a cousin who lived in Africa. She explained that he was gifted in prophetic ministry. He came to Canada for a visit, and she brought him to class to meet me. Upon arrival, he told her that he had a word from God for me.

We found a quiet place in the college to pray. He prophesied that I would write several spiritual books and travel the world as a renowned author.

The second event profoundly impacted me for years to come. One of my students was an older gentleman who had achieved multiple years of sobriety. He disclosed a social history riddled with horrific trauma and expressed that the class experience simulated a pseudo family. He was an outstanding student, a role model for his classmates. He often excelled over and above the curriculum expectations. He was noted for supporting classmates in their recovery outside of class time.

Near the end of his in-class term, I noticed him struggling. He expressed experiencing symptoms of separation anxiety and premature grief at the thought of leaving the classroom environment. During his last week of class, I had scheduled time off for a day surgery. On my way home from the hospital, I received a call from another student who was distraught and in a state of shock. She disclosed that this student had taken a gun and blown his heart out through an act of suicide!

Devastation rippled throughout both the addiction program and the campus as a whole. An outside source was brought in to facilitate a group debrief session in which over forty current and past students attended. I attended his funeral with the campus director, the director of the college, and several of his classmates. Shortly after his death, prayer groups broke out in a secular college and many people came to know the Lord. His imprint on life lives on in the hearts of many students and staff. His memory will profoundly impact me throughout the days of my life.

━━━━⟨∘⟩━━━━

Two years into my employment term, the campus director resigned. She accepted a campus director position at another college. One afternoon she invited me to lunch to discuss a proposition. She proposed that I attend a meeting with her in which we would present a sales pitch to the management team. The chief executive officer and the curricula manager attended the meeting. They listened as we proposed rolling out the design and development of an addiction worker program. Did I mention that her proposition entailed that I would head up the program design and development?

As I listened to her proposition, I was at a loss for words. All I could muster up to vocalize was that I felt completely incompetent for the task. Her response was, "I think you can do it!" Once again, God proceeded to open doors that I deemed impossible. And so the journey began.

Launching into my new position, I began to design the curriculum for the new addiction worker program. I worked alongside various management teams to design and implement the program rollout, which involved a litany of tasks. I assisted in completing an application to the Ministry of Education. I obtained letters of intent from community agencies that were willing to host interns. I began building community relationships and assisted marketing and sales teams. I designed the curriculum and maintained its development. I also developed the internship protocols and evaluation criteria.

The curriculum design involved a great deal of sacrifice and discipline. I had set up my computer desk in the alcove of the front bay window of my home. The window was surrounded by plants and had a view of the street. I spent countless hours enveloped in the enormous task of designing the addiction program curriculum. I would often find myself struggling with the necessary discipline required to stay on task. It was quite distracting to listen to the frequent rumble of motorcycles riding by my bay window day and night.

My eyes would grow weary as I read through hundreds of textbooks in search of the perfect match for each of the seventeen program modules. At last the day came when I typed the final keystroke of the seventeenth program module—the memory will forever be recorded in every cell of my body! Words cannot express the exhilarating experience of accomplishing such an enormous task! I recall feeling a joy exploding through every fibre of my being. As I danced in my living room, I yelled the words, "I did it!" The rollout was ready to commence, and my classroom was laid out for teaching.

As I reflect on the experience of completing the curriculum design, I pause to notice the correlation to writing this memoir. My prior experience with curriculum design encourages me to press on. I am determined to complete the writing of my first book. I long and ache to attain that familiar sensory experience as I envision typing the last word in my memoir.

My experiences during my term as faculty head and instructor are too numerous to note. Every student left a profound imprint on my heart and taught me more than they will ever know. Life is made of moments that can so often be overlooked in the busyness of life. In some ways, teaching enabled me to capture the importance of learning to stay present in each moment. I have learned that it is in the present moment that I am able to connect with God and others.

Every day we are bombarded by more than 60,000 thoughts that sporadically race through our minds. These thoughts compete for our attention and a point of entry into short- and long-term memory. Our thoughts are processed through filters that often distort and blur reality. We stream information from our environment through these filters and create a story, whether fictional or real, based on our past experience. Our story, of any given situation, can greatly affect the impact of our current experience and, in turn, alter the map guiding our life's journey.

Our emotional brain has no concept of time. I have spent many moments in therapy learning how to separate the data of a situation from the emotion. Learning to separate data from emotion helps to slow down the way I process information so that I can find truth and healing.

Research indicates that memory retention can be achieved at optimal levels through teaching others. My teaching experience confirmed that repeated review of the curriculum content greatly improved my ability to retain information and enlarge my knowledge base.

I designed the curriculum to simulate a residential treatment experience. My students' expression of their in-class experience demonstrated a correlation to treatment. Students often demonstrated initial resistance to attend class, followed by group formation and normalization midway and separation anxiety upon termination.

Throughout the duration of the in-class experience, students displayed an ebb and flow of emotional states as they implemented the knowledge attained by practically applying it in their personal lives. A range of emotional responses was exhibited as students experienced the parallel journey of personal growth and academia.

The nature of the addiction worker program afforded me the opportunity to incorporate several practical outreach activities. Of notable mention was an annual "Sleep-a-thon" outreach activity. Several students joined me in sleeping outside the chosen agency to raise awareness for homelessness. We also raised funds in support of the many worthy causes offered through the agency. This event drew the attention of the mayor, who sent a letter to the college commending the students for their exemplary efforts and demonstrated leadership.

I had the privilege of teaching hundreds of students during my ten-year term. I am blessed to have learned such valuable life lessons from some of the most incredible people on God's earth. Their transformation was metaphoric to that of caterpillars transforming into butterflies and launching out into a world that is beautifully enhanced by their presence.

After six years, I was finally afforded the opportunity to launch the addiction program at a local campus. I jumped at the opportunity to work closer to home.

The program launch lasted approximately one year and came to a devastating end with the announcement of my layoff! My world was rocked, and the news of my unemployed status brought with it a flood of emotions. *What will I do now? Where will I go? Why me?*

I had recently buried four loved ones, my beloved dog of fourteen years passed away, and now I had lost my career. To avoid sinking into a black hole of despair, I tried hard to accept that I was powerless over the situation. I was blessed to have received a financial payout, which carried me for the next four months, and then I was qualified to receive unemployment benefits for up to five months. I prayerfully decided to take time off. I allowed myself time to grieve and recover from the magnitude of loss. I also felt God nudging me to reapply to ministry school to pursue a deeper relationship with Him and attain university degrees.

Chapter 4

Setbacks, Hindrances, and God's Unfailing Love

As I pause to reflect, I become aware of so many setbacks and hindrances throughout my journey; setbacks that attempted to derail me. Unravelling the tapestry of my life, at times, feels like a daunting task as I wrestle to compose a congruent narrative. A precise timeline of events has been hindered by the effects of trauma; trauma has fragmented my memory into scattered pieces. As I attempt to reconstruct the crucial elements of my story, I return to an earlier time in my life.

It would be a glorified delusion to state that upon starting a journey in recovery, a red carpet rolls out, the clouds part, and an army of doves descend from heaven. Society often believes that an addict's problem is their drug of choice and that if an addict would just refrain from abusing their drug of choice, all would be well. This belief is, however, erroneous.

I did not use drugs to feel better. I used drugs to stop feeling bad. Drugs were my solution to a number of precipitating factors.

Addiction is rampant in our society because *it works*; it numbs our pain temporarily. Then, like a wild animal attempting to be tamed, it turns on us with a vengeance.

⚬⚬⚬

After my first year in recovery, I began to notice the *pink cloud affect* had dissipated and the reality of life was illuminated. At my one-year anniversary, a fellow addict said, "Recovery looks good on you, and now the work begins." At that time, I was baffled by attempts to decipher her comment. In hindsight, I realized the magnitude of truth that was rooted in her words.

⚬⚬⚬

At the core of every addiction is a deeply rooted pain. Addicts are driven by an incessant need to avoid such pain.

My first memory of this deeply rooted pain occurred when I had achieved two and a half years of sobriety. I experienced an overwhelming surge of painful emotions coupled with flash-backs of childhood abuse.

My capacity to develop healthy relationships was minimal. I noticed a historical pattern of attracting men who were emotionally unavailable and who demonstrated patterns of untreated addiction.

Deep-rooted pain led to an emotional breakdown, and I sought help at a one-week inpatient program. The program was a codependency program for the family members of addicts.

I felt confident that I had kept my children from visually witnessing the physical abuse I endured from Larry. During the codependency program, I watched a movie about domestic violence. I was devastated to learn that although my kids didn't see the abuse, they had heard it. Hearing a physical assault can often cause a deeper level of trauma.

———❦———

Another memory of deeply rooted pain occurred when I had achieved five years of sobriety. I was with Nick, and I began to feel a homicidal, explosive rage surfacing. The rage was triggered when I learned that Nick was secretly exploring pornographic material. His behaviour progressed to lusting after real women.

Up until this point in my life, I had depressed my emotional pain, which created an implosion of negative emotions. Triggered by Nick's sexual behaviour, I felt unable to control my pain; it had reached explosive levels. Riddled by fear of this unfamiliar emotional experience, I felt lost. I did not know how to cope.

I called a friend for help. He came to the house and spent several hours talking me down. He then put me in touch with a woman who would introduce me to a doctor specializing in anger management.

The following week I was on my way to meet the doctor. The referral to this doctor was instrumental in my transformation. Working with the doctor helped me experience freedom from years of emotional turmoil.

I attended the doctor's Anger, Rage, and Violation workshop. The workshop was held on a weekend with approximately twelve participants. On my way to the workshop, I felt a range of emotions, from anxiety to anticipation. During the workshop, I fell asleep a couple of times due to the overwhelming amount of information.

Near the end of the session on Saturday, I felt my anger begin to surface. I could feel it rise to the upper quadrant of my chest and stop as if a steel wall were blocking it from erupting. When it came time to demonstrate energy release work, I felt a surge of anger that caused all kinds of systemic reactions. Unable to contain the energy, I volunteered to participate in energy release work.

A heavy bag was placed horizontally on a floor mat in front of me. I slowly began to put tight-fitting gloves on and hesitantly picked up a tennis racket. I kneeled in front of the heavy bag and slowly raised the tennis racket above my head. I lowered the racket down until it made contact with the heavy bag. Feeling awkward and nervous, I began to laugh and felt doubtful about the energy release activity.

The doctor began taunting me to hit the heavy bag with force. Suddenly a fiery surge of rage came exploding down my arms and I began to engage the heavy bag with great force. Years of hurt, pain, and anger came rushing to the surface. I began to see visions and faces flash before my eyes. I screamed from the depth of my being. My shoulders and arms pierced with pain until all strength had been exhausted from my body.

When I finished the activity, I noticed I was weeping. My heart was racing, and I was shaking uncontrollably. Suddenly, I realized that my jean overalls were soaked with urine. I was full of shame and whispered, "Doctor, I just pissed my pants."

The doctor replied, "You are releasing years of toxins that have been locked within your body. This is normal. Some people vomit, some excrete feces, and some urinate. There is no judgment in this room. You are safe." He then asked permission to invite other participants to gently touch my shoulder as an act of loving kindness.

I finished the workshop weekend and was profoundly changed by the experience. The doctor encouraged me to attend his weekly process group. I agreed to attend.

I spent two years travelling four hours, round trip, to attend his process group. The emotional work I experienced in his group proved significant. I learned to manage life's emotional energy and to begin to heal from significant past traumas.

Eventually Nick attended the Anger, Rage, and Violation workshop with me as well a Communication workshop. I was, however, struggling to remain in the marriage due to his continued unacceptable sexual behaviour.

⌘

As well as my attendance at various therapy groups, I continued attending twelve-step meetings. During one particular twelve-step meeting, I met a man from California. He was introduced to the twelve-step recovery program by men who hung out with one of the co-founders of Alcoholics Anonymous. He began to guide me through the twelve-step program as outlined in the *Big Book of Alcoholics Anonymous*. Because of his indirect association with the cofounder, the recovery guidance I received was pure.

As I began to study the book, I felt as if it was written about me. The first forty-three pages in the book outlined the first of twelve steps and taught me about my disease. The second step helped me gain a deeper understanding of spirituality. The third step provided tools to aid me in becoming free from self-will by teaching me how to surrender to a Power greater than me. The fourth step involved writing an inventory of my resentments, fears, and past sexual behaviour. Through confession, the fifth step enabled me to recognize and be rid of old ideals and bitter toxins that had infected my mind, body, and soul for years.

Steps six and seven helped me to recognize my character defects, and I humbly asked God to take them all, root and branch. Steps eight and nine involved a process of direct and indirect amends in which I set out on a journey to right the harm I had caused others. Step ten taught me how to maintain healthy relationships with myself, with God, and with others. Step eleven took me on a journey through the discipline of prayer and meditation. I learned that conscious contact with God involved seeking Him with the desperation of a drowning woman. God of my understanding cannot be put in a box lined with rituals, religious stereotypes, or orthodox views.

God met me where I was at and used many recovered addicts to love me until I could love myself. I often sought God in nature or by the sea. The hypnotic sound of the waves or rhythmic whisper of wind in the leaves provided a safe haven and serene solitude.

Arriving at step twelve, I couldn't wait to carry the message to the still suffering addict entrenched in untreated addiction.

Having finished my step work, I attended a mediation meeting with Nick. That meeting was disastrous and ended with him acting out in a vocal fit of rage. I firmly announced I was leaving for good. Nick and I had separated for a few weeks in an effort to salvage what was left of our marriage. His outburst during the mediation meeting was the final straw.

I found an apartment and began packing my belongings. The moving date fell on my birthday. Shortly after my kids and I were settled into our new home, I heard the audible voice of God instruct me to remain there for exactly one year.

On moving day, Nick returned home unannounced and created quite the scene in front of my daughter and friends. Unmoved by his childlike display, I moved the last of my belongings and closed that chapter of my life.

My kids and I moved to a beautiful home located two blocks from a river. My son and I resided on the main floor, and my daughter, who was pregnant, lived in the upstairs apartment with her boyfriend.

The main floor apartment was beautiful, with wide antique hardwood flooring and a gas fireplace located next to a large bay window. The backyard was, once again, the epitome of heaven on earth, with a large, two-tier wooden deck overlooking a beautifully landscaped yard bordered by mature trees, magnificent gardens, and a wooden fence. Squirrels, chipmunks, and a litany of birds frequently visited this safe haven. I recall fond memories spent in the tranquility of the backyard.

Moving to this home brought a painful sacrifice. I had to sell my motorcycle in order to buy new furniture for my kids and me. I remember my daughter mentioning that I hadn't shed a tear when I left Nick but that I bawled tears of sorrow watching the departure of my Harley! It was in this home that I would finish writing the Addiction Worker program curriculum and launch into my ten-year career teaching numerous amazing students.

Shortly after moving, I began to receive threatening voice messages, which were disturbing to say the least. The messages entailed statements that involved someone threatening to "carve me like a fish" if I went near Nick again. The police were called, and a report was filed.

Following these threats, we had another disturbing occurrence. I was at a concert out of town when my daughter called stating she had heard a noise outside and the dog was barking. When she went downstairs to my apartment, she saw flames on the front porch that were as tall as the top window of the front door. Unable to return home in a timely manner, I called a male friend to go check on her and see what was going on at the house.

Returning home I noticed cigarette and cigar butts on the ground beside the side windows of the house.

That night, as we thought about what could have happened, my daughter and I experienced a brief period of fear-induced panic. Simultaneously, we turned to each other and declared that we refused to allow anyone to threaten or intimidate us. We immediately let go of our fear and did not experience any further threats or incidents from that day forward.

My daughter went into labour during the month of January. The birth of my grandson was an experience that demonstrated the power of God! In twenty-one days I was blessed to have experienced an entire cycle of death and birth. My grandmother had passed away on January first, and twenty-one days later, I witnessed the birth of my grandson.

The paradox of witnessing my daughter in excruciating pain in order to birth new life was an experience indescribable in words. Minutes before my grandson was born, my daughter had reached the point of exhaustion and expressed having no energy left to extend the final push needed to birth her son. In a state of fear and desperation, I attempted to piss her off, hoping that she would utilize her expression of anger toward me as an energy boost to make that final push. It worked. My beautiful grandson entered the world with a tiny cry, and my daughter relaxed into the hospital bed utterly exhausted.

My grandson continues to be a source of joy and blessing in my life.

Prior to selling my motorcycle, I began engaging in old patterns of behaviour. I hung out with old party friends and vowed to attend every motorcycle event that I had not had the opportunity to attend with Nick. Despite having a lot of fun, I had an intuitive sense that if I remained on this path, I would end up in the grips of active addiction.

Near the end of the summer, I chose to stop attending these social activities. Refraining from this lifestyle brought with it an emotional, withdrawal-like state.

Lowered emotions began to creep in. One night I was bombarded by thoughts of ending my life. I cried out to God for help. He orchestrated a divine encounter. My best friend came to my house and I shared a fifth step inventory specific to my past criminal involvement. I knew that a thorough housecleaning was necessary in order to maintain sobriety, but I was plagued by fear at the thought of such disclosure.

Facing my fear with a trusted friend allowed me to purge this final portion of my inventory, and I will never speak of it again. I felt assured that she would take my secrets to her grave. God, in His infinite wisdom, knows what I need before I do. I was finally free from the chains that bound me to the past.

As I near the end of writing this book, I feel ambivalent. Anxious thoughts flood my being. I feel like I am cracked wide open and in a vulnerable state. It isn't easy writing a memoir of my life and exposing the internal depths of my healing journey. One side of my ambivalence reveals an opportunity for healing and freedom as I purge the internal turmoil that has raged like a turbulent sea. The other side of my ambivalence shudders at the thought of birthing a story that I have kept hidden in the secret crevices of my soul. God continues to nudge me to finish writing. I will trust in His plan and pray that my healing journey will help others embrace their pain, knowing it is a necessary catapult to spiritual growth.

As the closing date for the purchase of my first home approached, my excitement was met with obstacles that attempted to steer me off track. I received a call from my lawyer who regretfully informed me that although I had never officially owned my own home, I did not qualify for the first time homeowner's discount because I had resided in the marital home with Nick. This and one other obstacle brought with it the added expense of a few thousand dollars—money I didn't have.

These obstacles triggered an emotional meltdown. I began to entertain thoughts of engaging in criminal activity to cover the costs. Thank God for good friends who quickly interrupted my train of thoughts and redirected me to ponder a spiritual solution to the situation.

I decided to be grateful that I had a line of credit and trusted God would make a way for me to pay off the added debt. Two months after moving into our new home, the furnace stopped working and again I had to rely on credit to purchase a new furnace.

On November 1st, I was able to move into my new home, thanks to hard work, faith, and a loan from my parents. This home opened the door to new beginnings for my children and me. It offered a secure, stable environment and peace of mind, knowing we could not be thrown to the curb as the result of another failed marriage.

God blessed me with a beautiful three-bedroom bungalow that included a two-bedroom in-law suite in the basement.

My daughter and her family resided in the in-law suite. My son and I resided on the main floor. I rented out the third bedroom to a boarder to maintain affordability. My dream home presented many blessings, including move-in ready living conditions.

I secured the deal on the house based on full-time hours at the college. For the first several months, I worked fourteen-hour days, including three hours of commute time. Shortly thereafter, my hours were cut to half days, which in turn resulted in a huge pay cut. Panic stricken and full of fear, I struggled to make ends meet.

During my recovery, I learned that God is either everything or He is nothing, so I surrendered my financial situation to God and trusted that He would make a way for me. Within a few months' time, the management team at the college informed me that we were rolling out the addiction program at another campus and my hours would be returning to full-time. God is good, all the time.

◦◦◦◦∞◦◦◦◦

For the next couple of years, my life ran smoothly. It was a welcomed reprieve from the steady onslaught of trials that bombarded my life. Roughly two years after buying my house, my daughter disclosed that her boyfriend was moving out. I was distraught about the news and heartbroken as I witnessed my little grandson crying and distressed when he saw his dad moving out.

The end of my daughter's relationship resulted in the loss of her vehicle. I experienced transference through my daughter as I recalled the amount of loss I had suffered through failed marriages. I had flashes of rage at the thought of my children and me being thrown to the curb.

I had to walk away from two marital homes because they were solely in my ex-husbands' names. There wasn't any equity to fight for. Driven by a need to protect my daughter from experiencing further pain, I bought her a car. She honoured repayment of the loan, and ironically, I felt a sense of healing from my past loss.

As I remember the visual image of my grandson in distress, I feel a slight pain in my heart coupled with an increased heart rate. I desperately long for my children to experience a healthy family system for both themselves and their children. I still feel a great deal of sadness. Occasionally, I fall privy to self-blame, believing that if I had modelled a healthy family system, perhaps their lives would be more stable. God, please forgive me. Please bless my children and grandchildren abundantly and watch over their comings and goings.

The demise of my daughter's relationship brought with it sporadic incidents of partying at the house. House parties and alcohol or drugs on my property were against our mutual agreement.

Previously, my children had been very respectful and supported my recovery by not bringing alcohol or drugs anywhere near my home. This sudden onset of parties at the house resulted in a stressful living environment, damage to the property, and frequent disagreements.

Both of my kids continued to engage in sporadic partying at the house. My son and I had a discussion about bringing alcohol into my area of the house and about coming home intoxicated. Eventually we mutually agreed that he needed to experience independent living.

My son accepted a job opportunity out west, moving to reside with his friend. I gave him a thousand dollars to help with start up and moving expenses. I wanted the best for my son and was proud of his courageous and adventurous spirit. The venture west did not go as planned. He moved home within a few months.

One of my favourite sayings is "I want my ceiling to be my children's floor." My interpretation of this is a desire to motivate my children to excel above my capabilities and achievements. I contributed by providing sustainable supports to help them achieve these standards.

My plan was to use equity from my first home to purchase a second home for my daughter followed by a third home for my son. In hindsight, I recognize that striving to fulfill my children's desires caused them to develop an unhealthy dependency on me and hindered their growth and independence. I also became so focused on being a good provider that I neglected to provide nurturing and at times was emotionally unavailable.

Sometimes children's plans don't line up with those of their parents. Sometimes situations in life reroute our plans.

A year or two after my daughter's relationship ended, she met another guy. Eventually, he moved in with her and the parties decreased substantially. My daughter began to experience chronic back pain and was introduced to narcotic pain meds. Over time, I observed her becoming dependent on pain medication and I felt anxious because of the highly addictive potential of narcotic analgesics.

My son is a very charming and handsome young man, which afforded him the opportunity to date many beautiful young girls. His first committed relationship, to my knowledge, was with a quiet, stunning young girl who came from a family of wealth. She demonstrated strong family values and a dedicated work ethic in her family's business. Her family offered my son a job and an opportunity to learn the family business. He was also invited to join them on a tropical vacation trip.

My son became very motivated to succeed in business and began applying to various colleges. Having been accepted by a well-known college, his grandfather co-signed a student credit line to support his post-secondary education. My son's relationship began to experience turmoil and eventually ended for reasons unknown to me. My son began to engage in partying again, assumedly to attempt to deal with his heartbreak.

Soon after his breakup, my son began to date another beautiful girl who exhibited strong family values. My son seemed to struggle with the idea of commitment. Their relationship ebbed and flowed with a pattern of break up and reconciliation. My son came to learn that his new girlfriend was pregnant with his child. He was passionately determined to be an amazing father to his child and made a decision to move in with his girlfriend. Her father agreed to rent them the main floor of his rental property. I gave them my living room furniture and a kitchen table set—I wanted him to have a nice home for his new family.

My son's girlfriend chose to give birth at home. She had a doula throughout her pregnancy and arranged the logistics for water birth. I attended the water birthing along with the rest of our families. My son was by her side for the entire process, and he did an amazing job of offering support and welcoming his beautiful daughter into the world—he even cut the umbilical cord. I was so proud of him.

I had raised my children solely on my own financial resources. I had a court order for child support enforced through the Family Responsibility Office. Larry's chronic history with addiction prevented him from securing a steady source of income. During one stint in prison, he learned that he could pursue a case with Veteran's Affairs for PTSD endured when he was in the army. Long story short—he received a settlement of several thousand dollars and a monthly pension (plus medical costs). I did not receive a penny toward his outstanding child support arrears.

When I called Larry to offer to work out a deal regarding child support arrears, he said, "Fuck you!" and hung up the phone. It was at this point that I decided I had extended enough energy over the years trying to help Larry by offering compassion and concern. Historically when I attempted to support Larry, he demonstrated a level of cordial behaviour. When I attempted to ask for financial assistance required to raise our children, he became hostile.

Larry served me with court papers several years later, a petition to wipe his child support arrears to zero. I had enough and decided to fight this in court. About a year later, I won the case! Larry finally agreed to pay $20,000 in arrears (the original order was for over $60,000) and the courts ordered payment on the arrears at the rate of $100 per month. I had succeeded in raising the kids on my own. At this point in my life, the court fight was about standing up to Larry and refusing to cower.

<hr>

As my daughter's relationship with her new boyfriend came to an end, she announced that he was moving out. From my perspective, how she chose to deal with the heartache was to numb her emotions through the use of alcohol. Her choice to sporadically engage in partying brought with it increased disagreements between us. My frustration was driven by fear. I longed for my daughter to have a better life than I did. I projected my internal fears in the form of nagging, obsessive worry, and attempts to control her behaviour.

⚜

It is difficult to welcome an optimistic future vision when holding onto past pessimism. My life's circumstances drove me to mirror parenting styles I had observed from my mother. In hindsight, I believe my mother's parenting intentions were positively motivated but greatly clouded by her own unresolved emotional issues. My mother wanted the best for me but attempted to live vicariously through me by means of control that manifested as continual guilt, shame, and negativity—all of which were driven by her fear and clouded by my addictive entrenchment.

Like my mother, I too held onto a pessimistic future vision, which was riddled with fear of ever attaining my desired future. I saw my future through a victim mentality. Pessimism drove me to hold onto the past and trapped me in a self-made prison—a prison that would take years to dismantle!

I learned it is extremely difficult to create a new reality when processing a self-image and worldview through distorted filters. I needed to find healthy role models that I could learn from and re-create my life. But first I was to plummet into another addiction that almost took me out. In attempts to fill the void and stop the incessant pain, I plummeted into the world of sex and love addiction.

⚜

At this point in my life, I had spent over twenty-five years in committed marriages. I felt I had sacrificed years of my life to loyalty, family, and raising children. I longed to experience what I perceived as an adventurous young adulthood. Many of my friends experienced independent living, travelling, dating, and post-secondary education (specifically university). Still feeling like I had missed out on many youthful experiences, I set out on a dangerous course of near self-destruction.

I was introduced to the world of online dating. I rationalized its authenticity by believing an ideology that I was too busy to find a God-filled man by natural means. Social media is riddled with invitations to dating via an internet vortex of dating websites. My curiosity got the better of me, and after a few promptings from friends, I joined the social norms.

Initially, I drowned out the warnings that clenched my gut by minimizing the potential dangers that lurked in the shadows. I experienced internal conflict as I entertained thoughts such as, "Everyone is doing it," "I am too busy to find a suitable partner," "I am older and don't drink so it's harder to find a good man," or "I can adjust my dating profile to reflect a desire to meet a Christian man." I finally took the leap into the online nightmare; little did I realize what awaited me.

Initially, I sought out "Christian" dating sites and even paid for registration fees. These dating sites were slow, boring, and uneventful, so I shut them down.

Addiction is a progressive illness and most often associated with substance abuse. Behavioural addictions are called "process addictions" and present in five main areas: gambling, eating disorders, workaholism, compulsive buying, and sex and love addiction.

I needed a dating site with a bit more "punch"—a greater adrenaline rush. I found one, and the switch for more was triggered. Within seconds of creating my profile, I was flooded by responses from men. As I delved deeper into the online vortex, I found myself spending hours in front of the computer. When that wasn't enough of a rush, I began accessing the portal from my cell phone so I could gain mobile accessibility.

I would check the portals at work, in the car, on social outings, and even while on dates with other guys. My behaviour became unmanageable, and I was out of control. I chased the next high as if intoxicated by a substance—the adrenaline rush was elusive.

The behaviour paralleled that of preparing to obtain an eight ball of cocaine. The onset of interest, the build up to the "hit," the let down when the date was devoid of connection, and the trigger for more kicked in. The rush of the first "hit" became harder to obtain, and the familiar systemic response of skin crawling associated with withdrawals stimulated a need for "one more." This vicious cycle came to a crashing end when the potential for self-demoralization smashed me in the face.

The majority of the dating prospects led to an initial coffee date with no chance of a second meet up. On occasion, I would afford a prospect a second date if I sensed a potential for connection. It wasn't long before my behavioural addiction led me to default behaviours. I began corresponding with the "bad boy" prospects.

After dating one bad boy for a few months, I faced a gruelling scare. Terror gripped my soul as I feared I had contracted a sexually transmitted infection. I was prescribed a very strong medication, as a precautionary measure, until the test results produced a diagnosis. The prescription had extreme negative side effects, and my emotional brain played havoc on my thought life. The day came when the test results proved negative, thank God!

That scare was a blessing in disguise—it afforded me the motivation to discontinue the self-destructive behaviour. I shut down all dating sites, social media, and email correspondence. I deleted every associated contact on my phone. I endured withdrawal symptoms. I applied the same spiritual principles used in recovery from substance abuse. I admitted complete defeat and surrendered all of my addictions to God.

The grace of God kept me from succumbing to a relapse with my drug of choice, but I was spiritually bankrupt and knew I had a lot of emotional growth work ahead of me.

One of my dating adventures took me to another country. Upon returning home from this nightmare, I felt depleted and emotionally exhausted.

Shortly after my return home, I received a call from a friend in recovery. He explained that he had a speaker cancel last minute and was in need of a favour. He wanted me to speak at a conference on the "Institution Panel."

I laughed and shook my head when I asked, "Why would you ask me to speak on an Institution Panel? I haven't done any long-term time in jail."

He replied, "Have you been detained in a jail cell and have you done any stints in any other types of institutions?"

I said, "Oh ya, I guess you got me there." So in my emotionally broken state, I agreed to help him out. God in His infinite wisdom and unmerited grace knows what we need before we do.

I drove to the conference, checked into the motel, and dragged my physical body to the event. I don't recall who was in attendance that night or a word that was spoken. I continually fought the urge to run and isolate myself in my motel room. Upon awakening, I picked up my phone and forced myself to go through the motions of prayer and meditation.

> *While writing this paragraph, I became aware of an internal voice telling me not to write the last sentence. Fear of judgment and criticism gripped me. An internal default mechanism quickly surfaced, manifesting as internal feelings of anger. I recited internal thoughts: "Who gives a rat's ass what those religious people think? Judge me lest ye be judged. Yes, I know how to recite scripture and play Bible bingo too. So I forced myself to meditate and recite prayers—so what, at least I am honest. I wear my emotions on my sleeve. I am not perfect. So what if I am a poor example of a 'good Christian girl.' I am honest and I am trying to do the next right thing. For this addict, that means I get honest with myself, God, and another human being."*
>
> *I realize my own personal growth as I write about my current feelings and internal dialogue. I calibrate the speed at which the dialogue comes and goes as if floating by on a cloud. I become aware that I no longer place emotional attachment to the thoughts but rather observe them float by. I sit with the observation for a few brief moments and then recognize my own judgment and criticism of "religiosity." I ask God to help me remain loving and tolerant of others and to free me from the bondage of self.*

I suited up accordingly for the conference events and made my way over to registration. God had plans for me beyond my wildest dreams, plans that would profoundly change the course of my life.

> *I take a deep breath and stare out my bedroom window as I prepare to write once again. We have just endured a long summer heat wave and early September has embarked with a brisk, cool*

fall like day. I can hear the wind chimes clanging to a new song as I watch the breeze sporadically dance through the trees creating a mesmerizing trance like experience. I fight the familiar sense of fatigue that embraces me with each initial tap of a keystroke on my computer. Like a child enduring a long car ride shouts, "Are we there yet?" so my mind recites the ritual question, "Are we done yet?"

I entered the conference and did not recognize a familiar face. I took a seat at the table assigned to me and endured the gruelling feeling of loneliness that gripped my soul. My heart greatly resisted the idea of speaking today because my thoughts were chaotic and my heart felt heavy laden. I said a quick prayer asking for the love of God to permeate my being. I took the stage and began to share my experience, strength, and hope. God continually uses my story to infiltrate a message of hope—He uses my message in spite of my emotional state.

After I had finished speaking, a newcomer told me that my story was inspirational. She then proceeded to ask if she could give my number to a friend—she felt her friend could help me. I was confused and at a loss for words. I had years of recovery yet could not deny my internal state of turmoil and pain. Hesitantly, I consented to her proposal. I also met a guy named James at the conference. James would come to play a significant role in my life for the following three years.

<hr>

The newcomer introduced me to a guy named Luke. Luke had several years clean and belonged to a twelve-step group in another city.

During my first encounter with Luke, I told him I didn't like him and thought he was slightly arrogant. He did, however, share something that intrigued me and left me wanting what he had. He shared that the negative, obsessive internal voices had ceased to infiltrate his thought life. My longing to obtain internal peace and serenity overcame my resistance. I was willing to begin working the steps with Luke and was hungry to acquire the serenity I witnessed in his life.

Over the next three years, I worked painstakingly to clear away the wreckage of my past. God used Luke to awaken my spirit at depths I did not deem possible. I learned that I had implemented half measures in many areas of spiritual surrender. I experienced a great deal of resistance when asked to let go of some of my character defects and default behaviours. In so doing, I learned I had an enormous amount of faith in God but I didn't trust Him. I would surrender one area of my life but continue to run the show by controlling other situations.

I held onto a victim mentally and continually blamed people, places, and situations for the pain and suffering in my life. Rarely was I willing to recognize where my actions caused chain reactions that produced self-induced suffering and caused harm to others. Luke taught me how complete surrender breaks the chains that bind us and complete trust in God produces freedom.

Willingness to admit complete defeat and surrender was a walk in the park compared to spiritual housecleaning. Taking a look at the wrong I had caused others was humiliating, to say the least. Becoming willing to clean up my side of the street and make amends required that I allow my ego to be smashed. I began to look at situations in my life from an entirely different perspective. For the first time in my life, I saw how my actions, choices, and behaviours hurt others. I began to see how resentments, fear, sex behaviours, and bitterness had hardened my heart. God did not abandon me—I shut Him out. I had built a twelve-foot steel-girded wall around me—a prison. I began to feel the love of God flow into my being as I walked out a process of "owning my shit" and asking others for forgiveness. I was reborn.

❦

As I began to apply the spiritual principles in all areas of my life, I began to experience an internal shift in awareness and connection to the Spirit of the universe. I felt fully alive. Having had a spiritual experience as the result of working the twelve-step recovery program, I was on fire. I had a burning desire to share my experience with others so they too could attain freedom from the binding chains of addictive behaviour and spiritual death.

Luke taught me that it was okay to acknowledge my femininity. He encouraged me to add colour to my life, and I slowly incorporated vibrant colours into my wardrobe and home decor. I began to wear dresses. I allowed God to break down the walls of rage and bitterness and welcomed feelings of vulnerability and humility. I became aware of how I used profanity to evoke fear and intimidation—a type of false pride and protection.

I adhered to Luke's suggestion regarding the sale of my Harley—even though at the onset his suggestion seemed ludicrous and indicative of brain damage *(laughing out loud)*. I had lost sight of "riding for God." Riding began to trigger an internal switch that attempted to reconstruct my ego and engage old default behaviours.

After two years without a bike, I began to rent bikes to attend the occasional ride. Slowly, I felt the hard exterior persona associated with riding being dismantled. I felt genuinely at peace with riding, and finally Luke agreed that I was finally in the right mindset to obtain another bike.

During the conference, I was introduced to a guy named James. The conference was breaking for lunch, and a friend asked if I wanted to go with him to his buddy's house for lunch. Not knowing many of the conference attendees, I complied. During lunch at James' house, I learned he had multiple years in recovery, was a teacher, and was very well known in the recovery circles. He was an active member of Cocaine Anonymous in the region, and I wanted to learn how to start a Cocaine Anonymous group so we exchanged phone numbers.

Unbeknownst to me, James had other motives for asking for my phone number. He called me about a week after the conference to ask me to speak at a Cocaine Anonymous meeting. I accepted his invitation to speak because I wanted to learn more about Cocaine Anonymous. After the speaking engagement, he asked me if I would like to go out to dinner. It was in that moment that I realized James had a personal agenda in obtaining my number.

Initially I hesitated to date James because he did not present as my usual dating type. He didn't ride a motorcycle, nor did he meet a bad boy criterion. He presented as upper class, educated, and an all-encompassing poster boy for the nice guy club.

The onset of our encounters was void of physical attraction, and it didn't appear we had much in common aside from our commonalities in recovery and teaching. Overcome with loneliness and with a dislike of the singles club, I succumbed to his dating proposal.

James and I dated off and on for about three years. I struggled a great deal throughout those three years as I learned to live outside of my comfort zone. I never felt like I fit in James' world. The upper class lifestyle was foreign in nature and awkward, to say the least. James introduced me to live theatre, elite social dinners and outings, attendance at the world's skating competition, fine dining, and fluid spending habits.

Historically, my role in relationships was that of caretaker, provider, and enabler. My past relationships were entrenched in violence, abuse, addictions, betrayal, affairs, sexual immorality, and a litany of criminal activities. The idea of belonging to upper class circles was just a vision encapsulated in a motion picture.

Entrapment in a poverty mindset is not broken through the attainment of wealth and material possessions but rather from a shift in perspective. Our thoughts create our reality.

For years I had felt unworthy of the life envisioned in childhood dreams—belonging to a healthy family system and free from abuse, brokenness, and financial indebtedness. It took me fifteen years in sobriety to clear away the financial wreckage of a $50,000 debt load. I attained financial freedom through a shift in perspective, hard work, and a vision.

※

Prior to meeting James, I had purchased my first home. Tired of being thrown to the curb after two failed marriages, I was determined to secure a home I could call my own. For a year, I worked fourteen-hour days at the college and endured the long commute.

My mom's encouragement to own my own home strengthened my determination. My parents endorsed my determination by lending me the down payment. Finally the day came when God rewarded my efforts and I was given the key to my new home. Turning the key for the first time marked a significant milestone in my journey. I had crossed the threshold to a new perspective and sense of security.

Throughout the three-year sporadic relationship with James, I learned that it is situationally appropriate to allow others to care for me. I learned that I am worthy and capable of living outside the barriers of an impoverished lifestyle. I came to see that, beyond the ambiance of wealth, people still struggled with the turbulence of life disguised beneath the projected portrayal of perfection.

We all travel an unprecedented continuum of life from birth to death, regardless of socio-economic class. Beneath our surface persona, we all face the commonalities of human existence—we are spiritual beings embodied in physical form, and we survive through maintenance of necessary physiological needs and aspire to connect and belong to a loving community.

I grew tremendously while in the relationship with James. I became aware of an internal duality that created a stuck point between a life I abhorred and a life I longed to acquire. I began the daunting task of learning to recognize and embrace my internal beauty versus fixating on a superficial exterior to manipulate my external facade. The relationship mirrored deeper truths about myself, which began to pave the way to spiritual growth.

In hindsight, I realize that James and I were much better suited as social companions versus intimate partners. During the first year of our relationship, I learned of James' addiction to pornography. I began to observe behaviours involving demonstrations of lust toward other women. Witnessing his behaviours unleashed a well of familiar internal pain that began to ooze a volcanic eruption of jealousy and insecurity. Fuelled by self-protective rage, I triggered a vicious cycle of breakup and reconciliation. During periods of breakup, I would rebel by seeking other men to fill the void. This pattern of pleasure seeking would later lead to a destructive sex and love addiction.

During one of our first breakups, tension was building at home between my son and me. In desperation, I reached out to James, seeking solace from my despair. James came to the rescue. He invited my son to reside with him. James' act of kindness masked a hidden motivation to reconcile our relationship—it worked for a while. My son stayed with him for about a year before returning to his hometown to live with his girlfriend. Once again, James and I went our separate ways.

On this occasion we remained estranged for several months—a timeframe that would bring with it two significant losses that would deeply impact the way I viewed the world.

Chapter 5

The Depths of Grief and Loss

My mother had endured fifteen years of suffering due to renal failure. A prior diagnosis of polycystic kidney disease led to a slow, chronic demise of her systemic functions. She became chained to a dialysis machine three to five times a week—five to six hours per visit.

Dialysis patients, on average, can sustain about ten years of dialysis before facing the destined outcome of "kidney transplant or death." During the later years of dialysis, the process fails to maintain the ability to remove toxins from the extremities furthest away from the heart. As the result of toxins remaining in the body, the systemic ability to heal breaks down. Hence, due to a litany of issues, a person can fail to be a suitable candidate for a kidney transplant.

The toxins in my mother's extremities eventually failed to be filtered through the dialysis process. This resulted in multiple unhealed wounds, gangrene, and eventually leg amputation. Amputation resulted in mobility issues that bound her to a wheelchair, which added unforeseen financial burdens and distress.

My parents were forced to sell their three-level, semi-detached home and purchase a bungalow that would allow main floor access to all amenities. Renovations were needed to allow for a wheelchair-accessible bathroom and exterior access ramps. The leg amputation also added to my mother's struggle with extreme chronic pain and emotional distress.

It is my personal belief that if we fail to work on our emotional issues, we internalize the negative energy, and eventually this energy produces toxins that poison our body—remember, "our thoughts create our reality." The energy of trauma and negative emotions are stored in billions of cells that sustain our body. I have experienced being trapped in negative emotional states. Negative thought patterns birthed negative behavioural states. Negative behavioural patterns manifested as unhealthy eating, lack of exercise, weight gain, low self-esteem, isolation, addiction, and various mental health issues. These negative patterns can produce a breeding ground for chronic illness and disease.

In seeking validity to my ideology, I researched a chronic disease (cancer) and learned that cancer cells cannot survive in an alkaline environment. Eating healthy food creates an alkaline environment. Acidic environments are created through ingestion of unhealthy processed foods.

It was heart-wrenching to witness my mother endure the litany of issues surrounding her battle with chronic renal failure. Her entire life became enveloped in the many aspects of living with chronic illness. From my perspective, she became her disease.

Many people have felt it is easier to accept the death of a loved one who has suffered for years with chronic illness versus sudden death. I disagree. In my experience, nothing prepares you for death of a loved one.

I watched my mother suffer for fifteen years. She endured excruciating pain, emotional distress, fear, depression, anger, and utter dependence on others for survival. I watched her disease eat her from the inside out. She experienced weight loss, muscle deterioration, vision loss, tooth decay, and amputation of both her legs. Near the end of her battle, she was diagnosed as borderline diabetic. She was at risk of her fistula failing—this is the medical procedure that allows dialysis treatment. And she lost control of her bowel and urine functions.

Every time my parents' number displayed on my phone, I felt my heart skip a beat. *Is this the call?* Chronic illness creates a ripple effect of emotional distress on the entire family system. It consumed our thoughts, conversations, and lifestyle. I can't even begin to explain the effects of chronic illness on the family system, especially to someone who has never experienced the heartache. I pray that each of you reading this memoir never has to endure such travesty.

In September of 2013, the call came. I was working at the college when my sister called to say that the hospital was notifying the family that Mom was in ICU and didn't have long to live. I hung up the phone in shock. The reality of her pending death hit me like a ton of bricks. I scrambled to find someone who could drive me to the hospital. God in His infinite wisdom orchestrated the arrangements. A student had her car in for repairs and was able to drive my car to the hospital.

The trek from work to the hospital was excruciating. So many thoughts, questions, and memories flooded my mind. Anxiety and panic manifested in systemic effects. I wasn't prepared for my mother's final breath.

As I recall the events of the days preceding my mother's death I feel an internal resistance to share the experience in written form. A familiar numbing encompasses my body, and my mind seems void of thought, as if I have hit the pause button. I stare at the computer screen, my fingers tap the keys, but there doesn't seem to be a connection between my cognitive functions and fine motor skills.

As I approached the door to my mother's room, I felt light-headed and experienced a shortness of breath. She lay before me in a coma. My father and sister were by her side. My brother-in-law and aunt soon joined us. We all sat around her bed sharing memories as we anticipated her final moments on earth.

As we embraced and celebrated her life, I began to hear classical music. At first mention of the music, my family thought I was delusional—hearing music that didn't exist. Then they too heard the sound of classical music. We weren't sure where it was coming from, and at one point, I wondered if we had all been transported to heaven with my mother! My mother loved classical music.

Finally I had enough of the mystical ambiance and asked the head nurse about the source of the music. The nurse confirmed there was music playing. The hospital had acquired expensive ICU beds that had speakers embedded in the head of each bed. The nurse decided to play classical music for my mother, stating she believes patients in a coma can still engage auditory functions. Upon further research, I learned that auditory function is the last sensory experience to go prior to death.

My sister, father, and I spent the first night asleep by her side. The next three nights, only my father and I remained. On the fourth night, a nurse entered the room around 1:00 a.m. to awaken my father. She encouraged him to say his final goodbye because her death was near. As I watched my father by my mother's bedside, I felt the experience was surreal. I observed the next series of events as if through the lens of a movie camera.

My mother took her last breath. My father went into a state of shock. He kept gripping her jaw in attempt to close her mouth. He banged on the monitors and machines surrounding her bed. His voice was childlike in nature with the resemblance of my grandfather's tone. He looked at me and repeatedly asked, "What am I going to do now?" I just stared blankly at the motions.

Not one tear fell from my eyes—the shock was intense. All I could bring myself to do was encourage him to call his older brother. I dialled the number and listened to his conversation. My uncle's response sounded void of emotion, and my father hung up the phone.

Unable to witness my father's pain, I told him I would give him a few moments alone with Mom and proceeded to leave the room. On my way out of the room, a nurse stopped to ask if I was okay. I said, "No." She informed me that I was in shock and told me it's okay to express my pain. I found myself telling her I had to be strong for everyone.

The brisk morning air hit my face, and I welcomed the sensation. Grabbing my phone, I called my closest friend. She answered the phone, and I broke down as I said, "Mom is gone." We wept together as waves of emotion poured from my eyes. Returning to the room, I called my daughter and aunt to inform them that Mom had died.

My daughter entered the room and broke down hysterically. I embraced her in my arms as she wept at the sight of her grandmother's lifeless body. As I held my daughter, I felt fear gripping my entire being. I didn't know how to deal with the depth of loss, nor did I know how to nurture and comfort my daughter. Suddenly while embracing my daughter's pain, I realized I had spent my child-rearing days so enveloped in protecting and providing for my children that I had neglected to offer nurturing and support. This reality gripped the depth of my soul with regrets, shame, and fear. It is still difficult for me to extend nurturing to others because I was not modelled this type of behaviour in childhood—it was foreign in nature.

My son dealt with the loss by consuming alcohol so he was unable to make it to the hospital to say goodbye. Regret still haunts him despite my attempts to offer comfort.

My father, sister, and I stood around my mother's bed to say our final goodbyes. My father encouraged me to say goodbye. All I could muster up to say was, "We never even got to have a pedicure together." I have always felt this was a bizarre statement. My ability to numb the pain finally broke, and an overwhelming rush of emotional pain poured from my eyes. We left the hospital and returned to my parents' house.

Upon arrival at my parents' house, my son, who was intoxicated and emotionally distraught, greeted me. I felt like an emotional rag doll and hadn't an ounce of energy to extend as comfort—I was spent. Attempting to hold myself together, I asked him several times to stop drinking and go to bed. Caught up in his own grief and sadness, he ignored my request. Finally, I exploded in verbal distress and screamed, "I know you just lost your grandmother, and I am sorry, but I have nothing to give in this moment. I just lost my mother, now go to bed. We'll talk in the morning!"

<hr />

My memory of the next several days is a blur. I was a part-time employee at the college. Due to lack of medical benefits and bereavement days, I had to return to work the day after my mother's death. Over the years, I had developed excellent dissociative skills, which is how I coped at work until her funeral.

Sitting in the front pew of the funeral home, I was unprepared for the experience of burying my mother. She was only sixty-six years old—too young to die. My children were on either side of me with their arms embracing me as my body shook and tears poured from my eyes.

I recall her funeral as though observing it from a chair in a movie theatre. I see myself standing at the podium reading a dedication to her life. The long fitted black dress and black shawl draped over my shoulders could not hide the violent body tremors. I can see my father weep as I read the words emanating from my heart's gripping pain. I see my kids' father gripping his face in an attempt to hide his emotional struggle. I see myself resume my space on the pew between my children and cup my face in hopes I'd awaken from a nightmare.

The funeral service ended, and we endured the long drive to the gravesite. Only my immediate family attended the gravesite memorial. The experience at the grave felt cold and shallow. I was irritated with the funeral home because they chose a vessel for my mom's ashes that did not fit into the grave plot. They proceeded to explain the dilemma to my father, who authorized her ashes to be poured into a container that would fit the plot. They then proceeded to pour her ashes into the container, and I witnessed the wind capturing some of her remains and blowing them abroad. I was deeply distressed with the visual observation and had great difficulty comprehending the reality that this was all that remained of my mother. We stood in silence as the minister said the final regards, and then it was done.

As we stood in silence, I looked around and observed that I was the only family member who was crying. For a brief moment, I felt embarrassed then quickly accepted that people process grief differently. We left the gravesite and drove back to my parents' home to join family and friends for a time of celebrating Mom's life. After a few hours, I felt overwhelmed, and although I didn't want to be alone in this moment, I couldn't be around people any longer. I excused myself and went home.

The house was quiet and felt cold. I curled up on my couch in the fetal position. I heard my daughter come home and go downstairs to her apartment. I longed to be held by a loving, caring man, but I was single. I felt alone and empty in my grief.

I wasn't hungry but knew I needed to eat. I put a pot of soup on the stove and returned to the couch. Suddenly, the smoke detector sounded and upon returning to the kitchen I observed the stove in flames. I attempted to scream for my daughter but only a whisper emanated from my voice. My daughter ran upstairs screaming at me to put out the fire, but I was in a frozen, childlike state—unable to move or speak. I watched as she took a steel lid and put out the fire. I heard her say, "Mom, what is wrong with you? Snap out of it. You could have burnt the house down."

I wept, apologized, and said, "I don't know what's wrong with me." She went downstairs and I spent the remainder of the night crying myself to sleep, alone and gripped with unfathomable pain.

<hr/>

The irony in death is that life for those remaining must resume. My life, as I knew it, forever changed after the death of my mother. It's as though time stood still, and in the stillness, I pondered the familiar spiritual questions: Where did I come from? Why am I here? Where am I going? My spirituality was shaken to the core. Death challenged my own mortality. Fear gripped my soul, and life didn't seem to make sense.

My worldview changed significantly. I saw the world as if in a hazy vortex, whirling around at uncontrollable speeds. Millions of people busily travelling a daily ritualistic journey—destination "nowhere." Where was everyone going? It felt as though my visual perception was in slow motion but the external world was travelling at the speed of light. In hindsight, I believe my life began the day my mother's dash ended.

After my mother's death, I found it very difficult to cope with life. I attended grief counselling and returned to therapy. One of the most profound things I learned through my grief group was that the cliché "time heals all wounds" is erroneous. Time does not heal the wounds of loss; you just to learn to live without your loved one.

One night while seeking spiritual support from friends, a well-intentioned girlfriend attempted to correct a perception I had about where we go when we die.

My understanding had always been that if we are a believer in Christ, we go to be with Him in heaven. My friend began to explain that my mother wasn't in heaven; she was in a "dormant state." I lost my shit! I would not accept that my mother's body was decaying and her spirit lay dormant in some cold, black, void-like state. Believing that all dead believers are laying dormant until the rapture was just inconceivable to me.

I sought further spiritual counsel to seek comfort and relief from deep spiritual distress. A spiritual advisor provided comfort. She affirmed that after death, believers do not experience oblivion or sleep or unconsciousness but rather have an intimate, sweet experience of being immediately in Christ's presence.

Upon personal research, I learned that the biblical story of Lazarus and the rich man depicts what I choose to believe; my mom was safe in Christ's presence at the moment of her death. I also researched several personal stories of those who shared about their near-death experiences. Many shared personal accounts of immediate encounters with Christ. They expressed encounters that were so magnificent that they found it challenging to return to life on earth. Many expressed returning only to be with loved ones.

Approximately six months had passed since my mother's death, and I received another life-changing call. I was up north at a workshop with a few of my students. My son called and asked if I was sitting down. My heart raced. I sat down and entertained catastrophic thoughts in which I envisioned my son's dad had died. My son explained that my grand-daughter (my stepson's daughter) had been in a tragic accident and they weren't sure she would make it. Once again I experienced surreal levels of shock. My student and her husband offered to drive me to the hospital, which was almost three hours away.

The trek to the hospital was a three-hour drive but felt like a day's journey. As I gazed out the passenger window, so many thoughts and questions flooded my mind. *What happened? Why was this devastating tragedy happening to a young child? How is my stepson doing? Where is God in this situation?*

My son explained that a car had accelerated in reverse and crashed into huge glass doors of a local retail store. The impact of the car sent my granddaughter, her mother, and her sister flying about thirty-five feet in the air through the glass doors. I had great difficulty fathoming such a devastating tragedy.

My phone rang when we were about half an hour from the hospital. My son's tone was low and he began to choke up as he told me, "She didn't make it, Mom." I hung up the phone and sat speechless. I felt numb and in shock as tears streamed down my cheeks.

The silence broke when my student's wife said, "Look," and pointed up to the sky. The sky before us was cloudy and overcast. Suddenly a break in the clouds appeared, creating a stretch of radiant blue sky through which the most beautiful, vibrant rainbow illuminated the horizon. My body became full of goose bumps, and a wave of peace overcame me. I had a deep knowing that this symbolism was from my granddaughter. I would later learn that the rainbow offered a great deal of comfort and significance for my stepson.

<hr/>

We arrived at the hospital to find a group of family members standing outside in the smoking area. I walked toward them and spotted my stepson. He walked toward me and fell into my arms, weeping uncontrollably. I embraced him in silence. The tragedy remained surreal.

As the following weeks unfolded, I found it very difficult to express the impact of the devastating experience in mere words. The only way to explain the experience is to express that it felt as though I was "in a movie" and "watching a movie" at the same time. The tragedy was flooding the national media.

How do we comprehend the death of a young child? How do parents move forward after the loss of their child? I don't know. What I do know is that I was so deeply moved and proud of my stepson. His demonstrations of forgiveness, love, and compassion brought me to tears several times. He embraced his daughter's life as a celebration. Through his grief, he celebrated the life of his amazingly beautiful, passionate daughter. She had a zeal for life that radiantly impacted the nations.

There aren't any life manuals that teach us how to deal with grief and loss. One important lesson I have learned from dealing with death is that my experience is unique to me—I spiral downward when I compare my experience to that of others.

In the twelve-step program, we are encouraged not to compare our insides to another's outsides. When I succumb to this behaviour, it results in negative self-criticism and self-loathing, often resulting in a slow spiritual death. We learn to "identify" versus compare. The only healthy comparison is one that I use to identify my own personal growth.

I began to learn that pain was my greatest teacher and motivator for change. In the Bible, there is a guy named Paul who was noted as having a thorn in the flesh. We are not made aware of the specific nature of the thorn in his side. Does it really matter what specifically the thorn was? I think not. When I envision a thorn in my side, I immediately equate the experience to that of physical pain.

Life has taught me that I have an innate reaction to draw near to God when I experience the grips of fear and pain. For most of my life, I attempted to resist pain at all costs. Resistance created a paradox—greater resistance equalled greater pain. When I learned to accept pain and face fear, I began to embark on a healing journey.

As an addict, I learned that the only way to get to the other side of hell was to go through it, through the pain to spiritual growth. Maybe Paul's thorn in the flesh was a blessing and not a curse? Maybe my journey in active addiction was a blessing—a thorn in my side—ever reminding me that the essence of life and recovery is contingent on my willingness to maintain constant contact with God, as I understand Him.

As I reread this last sentence, the essence of life, I suddenly became emotional and felt tears well up in my eyes. Maybe I am finally starting to connect my intellect to my heart? Something about the word essence *resonated deeply within my spirit. The teacher/researcher voice in me said, "Look up the word* essence.*"*

Essence is defined as: being the intrinsic (belonging naturally, essential) nature of something that determines its character. The essence of life is defined as one's innate (natural) characteristics, quality, and substance of thoughts and actions. This brief research is awakening a reality that I have struggled with for years: it is difficult to know one's innate characteristics when void of childhood memory due to a chronic history of trauma. I don't know what I don't know.

How can we know where we are going if we don't have a point of origin? Multiple years of lived experience in therapy (encompassing a litany of modalities) has allowed me to become aware of a glaring gap in the therapeutic skill set. It has been my experience that very few doctors and therapists have the ability to navigate me through the "how" component of healing. Many could navigate me through a therapeutic archeological dig (which, by the way, I did not find very useful—I am not interested in being retraumatized), and many could navigate me through visualization of my ideal self. However, few could provide guidance in the navigation required to get from point A to point B—the how.

I have come to realize, through my own lived experience as an addiction counsellor, that it is not a therapist's responsibility to determine an individual's how.

The twelve-step program speaks about "re-creating one's life." Re-creation has been a key component in my recovery journey. Re-creation did not require me to remember my childhood, nor did it require an origin of sorts. Re-creation required connection to a Power greater than myself. Re-creation involved finding answers to the question, "Who do you want to be?" The therapy question, "Who are you?" was not useful in my healing journey.

Recovery has involved an intrinsic personal healing journey that I have learned to embrace alone with God. God has placed loving people to guide me along the way, but like birth and death, the journey is my responsibility. I am not sure how I got on this rabbit trail (laughing out loud), but I just went with it—God will reveal more to me as I go, and He directs my words.

After my granddaughter's death, I sunk into a depression and became increasingly unable to care for myself. I made a decision to rent out my house and move in with James. Resistance encompassed this decision, but I knew I was grief-stricken and unable to care for myself. Deeming myself a strong, independent woman, I did not invite words associated with vulnerability and surrender into my vocabulary. Needless to say, this decision was not within my comfort zone.

Upon commencing to pack up my personal belongings, I chose to move belongings from my office first. This choice was based on awareness of my past patterns of behaviour. Predictably, I experienced negative self-talk that manifested as second guessing my decisions and filled me with self-doubt. My office belongings contained about ten boxes full of heavy textbooks. My logic was it was less likely that I would change my mind after moving ten heavy boxes.

The move was complete, and depression intensified. I had expectations that this new life would involve alone time for me while James worked an eight-hour day and outside of that we would work on building a life together. My expectations proved delusional.

Reality unveiled a gruelling awakening into the depths of being alone with myself. Day after day I was alone with myself for fourteen hours a day. All of my belongings were crammed into two small rooms. I was tripping over furniture and felt like I lived in a hoarder's environment. My obsessive-compulsive disorder was rocketed into the fourth dimension. My daily routine involved waking up, drinking multiple cups of coffee, and going out on the front porch to chain smoke. In between cigarettes, I would walk the short distance back to resume my position in my bed, which was temporarily set up in the cramped living room quarters.

I was in a new city, one hundred kilometres away from all of my family and friends. I experienced daily anxiety, panic attacks, and social phobia. I neglected my self-care and lost all desire to venture outside of my home. Crying became a part of my daily routine. I had never experienced the depths of depression, loneliness, and isolation that gripped my being.

My thoughts were consumed with negativity, remorse, regret, and self-loathing. Every skill I implemented in an effort to keep me out of the grips of depression had failed. The winter winds raged outside, hindering any hope of connecting to my supports back home. A black cloud of despair began to close in around me as if metaphorically pushing me into the gates of hell. A small glimmering light within ignited enough strength to step outside the house long enough to see a doctor. I surrendered my will and accepted short-term pharmacological help through a low-dose antidepressant medication.

The dark clouds around me began to dissipate to that of an occasional sensation of heaviness. I mustered up the strength to attend a local twelve-step meeting. Recommitting to daily attendance at meetings allowed me to recognize that my ego had reconstructed and was manifesting through anger and resentments. I was very well known in the recovery rooms back home, but here I was welcomed as a newcomer. *Don't they know who I am?* became an internal question that screamed through my thoughts.

I called my sponsor to vent. He encouraged me to attend a Big Book meeting put on by old-timers. He told me to "bring a walker" and then abruptly hung up the phone. *What an ass-hole* became a frequent internal thought.

At one of my daily morning meetings, I was to meet a girl from another city. She would prove to be instrumental in interrupting the engagement of self-sabotaging behaviour. My concern for her wellbeing was the nudge I needed to get out of self. My internal flame of hope began to grow.

I am returning from a break from writing (yes, I had a cigarette, and yes, I am aware I need to quit, laughing out loud). While on break, God downloaded a metaphor about the recovery journey.

Recovery is like taking a journey into the wilderness. When preparing for a wilderness journey, an individual requires a backpack of survival tools. Seeking wisdom from forerunners who have endured a similar wilderness journey is essential. The forerunners recommend certain tools needed to endure the possible trials and tribulations that could present as obstacles along the path. The individual gathers the required tools and seeks guidance from those who have survived the trek. Securing the backpack over their shoulders, they head out on an unknown journey into the wilderness. The path is narrow and scarcely travelled. Although the survival tools are similar, it is unknown what tools will be utilized for each potential situation or how and when they will be needed. Each journey is unique, and no one can predict the varied potential obstacles. Not all will complete the journey, but each journey (whether completed or not) is a lesson for those who follow.

The flame ignited a hunger for a new level of recovery. Recalling a truth outlined in the program of recovery, I decided to attend meetings at another fellowship in search of new girls to work with. Our recovery program outlines an experiential truth, "When all else fails, work with another addict will save the day." When I attended the other fellowship, I challenged myself to engage a new attitude.

My sharing involved a cry for help. I shared that I was dying inside and in desperate need of new girls to work with. After the meeting, I had several girls approach me and within a week I was working with two new sponsees. My daily routine began to change. My new girls became a lifeline.

One of my new girls had a background in personal training and invited me to attend her gym. I would meet my girls at the gym and then go for coffee and take them through the twelve steps. I began to implement self-care back into my daily routine and expanded attendance at meetings to twice daily. My appetite returned, and social phobia subsided. As the isolating grips of winter began to lift, I felt a renewed hope and joy.

James and I decided to sell his house and purchase a new home so I could be closer to my family and work. When I moved in with James, I had taken a medical leave from the college. My medical leave was coming to an end, and I was not prepared to engage in a two-hour commute.

We bought a beautiful custom-designed home and secured a closing date in April. I came to learn that James had re-engaged his sexual behaviours and was acting out through pornography and lusting after various women. After a great deal of stressful arguments, we came to an agreement to wipe the slate clean and view the move as a new beginning. His sexual behaviours ceased for about six months after the move. Upon learning he chose to engage the behaviours yet again, I decided to end the relationship and move back to my home.

Shortly before ending the relationship with James, I had embarked on a new therapy experience. I met a doctor who was starting his own practice in psychotherapy. I was his first patient. Coming from a background as a medical doctor, I admired his insight into the systemic effects of trauma, cognitive function, and addiction on the nervous system.

This doctor has been instrumental in my healing journey. I have grown to maintain deep respect and gratitude for his gifted ability to guide me in developing "who I want to be."

During one therapy session, he noted that I was his most resistant patient. To which I responded, laughing, "What do you mean by that?"

He remains my therapist today, and I have come to welcome his candidness and embrace his challenges.

The division of assets with James didn't come without a fair share of stress and resentment, but finally the legalities were finalized and I moved home. The first month home involved cramped quarters because I still had a house full of boarders. The boarder occupying my master bedroom moved out, and I settled back into the comfort and safety of a familiar environment.

⁓⦇✖⦈⁓

I moved home in October. Christmas lay around the corner. I did not welcome the first "real" Christmas since my mother's death. I was also quite ambivalent about the idea of being single at my age. Most of my friends were married or in a committed relationship, so I felt isolated and alone again. I was willing to embrace new beginnings and take time to learn who I wanted to be. What I didn't see coming was a hidden addiction, which would reveal itself in the coming months—sex and love addiction.

⁓⦇✖⦈⁓

About a year after my mother's death, I experienced another tragic death that absolutely rocked my world and challenged the core of my being. I was babysitting my grandson because my daughter had a medical appointment. The phone rang, and it was my dad calling. His vocal tone was soft and his rhythm sporadic as he said, "Jenny is dead."

I said, "Jenny who?"

He responded, "Jenny, your cousin."

My body began to shake and my heart rate increased. Responding in disbelief, I told him this must be untrue because she was on her honeymoon in another country. My dad repeatedly insisted that I call my aunt.

I called my aunt and within thirty minutes I was en route to join the rest of our family. As I entered the room where the family was gathered, I observed a state of shock and disbelief resonating from each of their faces. A lot can be learned about the essence of life and the insignificance of time when in the midst of acute crisis.

Jenny was one of my closest family members; she was like a sister to me. We had a long history of adventures together, which depicted typical sibling attributes, including sibling rivalry. I embrace many fond memories in both our childhood and adulthood years. Of the treasured memories, those that highlighted my heart's passion were our riding adventures. We both loved to ride our Harleys together and could often be seen racing side by side on the open roads, feeling the wind in our hair and the freedom of nature's embrace as we sped off to destinations unknown.

Like most siblings, we fought on occasion. Our disagreements were often about trivial issues and could result in lack of communication for several months. Did I mention we were both very stubborn?

One of our disagreements involved a triviality in which we both dug in our heals and became uncommunicative with each other for months. A mutual friend finally intervened in our stubborn streak and coordinated mediation by way of a barbeque dinner. Much of life's precious moments can be squandered in petty, prideful disputes. In the blink of an eye, months of hard heartedness melted away and we regained our closeness and passion for mutual endearment.

It is gravely important to walk through life with a pure heart that doesn't harbour resentments. One never knows when our time is up. I am so grateful that I have an amazing twelve-step program that taught me spiritual principles, which have enabled me to live life without regret.

A week before my cousin left for her honeymoon, God put a strong urgency on my heart to go see her. One day the urgency was so strong, I could not resist nor avoid it. I went to visit her at work, which would prove to be the last time I would ever see her alive. Jenny and I had a wonderful visit. She invited me to attend dinner at her place on Christmas Day, and then I wished her safe travels. I hugged her goodbye; unbeknownst to me that this would be our last embrace! I was looking forward to hearing about her honeymoon upon her return, but that reality was smashed when she returned in a box.

In December 2014, my closest family member died at the young age of forty-five. Her funeral was several weeks after her death due to the red tape involved in an out-of-country death.

As I write about the tragedy concerning my cousin's death, I feel frustrated and discouraged because words cannot capture the depth of my despair and grief. I feel my words do not even begin to capture the significance of the loss. I also sense an internal numbing coupled with a resistance to write. I wish I could telepathically download words on the paper that would accurately capture the paradox of tragedy and beauty embracing the fragility of her life.

During the drive to the funeral home, I experienced an internal battle raging. One minute I felt waves of explosive anxiety surfacing, the next minute I would be overcome with an overwhelming numbness that seemed to block the reality of her death.

Arriving at the funeral home, my anxiety had reached astronomical levels; my body shook and I found it difficult to breathe. Stepping from the car, I observed a lineup of people extending out through the front doors. I paused to capture the surreal essence of the experience. Fear enveloped me as I struggled to find the strength to take a step toward the door. The sounds and movement from others seemed acutely amplified and in slow motion. The line began to move, and with every step closer to her viewing, I felt feeble and weak, uncertain if my legs would continue to support my body. I began to see family members but was unable to acknowledge or greet them. I was finally next in line.

I paused to capture the reality of her lifeless body lying before me in a coffin. My legs began to shake violently. My body weakened. Standing beside her coffin, my legs collapsed as I uttered a deafening scream and began to weep uncontrollably. The room became eerily silent as the utterance of weeping echoed throughout the room. My friends supported my body as I stared aimlessly, in gut-wrenching pain. After what seemed like eternity, I heard Jenny's husband's voice. My friends supported my body as I hobbled over to greet him. Falling into his arms, he embraced my trembling body. I needed fresh air. The room felt like it was closing in on me. Still weeping, I made my way through the crowds to the front door. I gasped as the cool air filled my lungs.

Numerous people attempted to offer support and condolences, but no amount of kindness relieved the painful void. As the viewing came to an end, the family joined around her to say our final goodbyes.

The funeral service was held at a large church due to the volume of attendees. A few years prior to her death, my cousin had made me promise that I would ensure we ride to her burial—even if she died in the winter months. I recall being very upset with the conversation, not wanting to engage in discussions about death. In hindsight I have wondered if she knew her time on this earth would be short. Did she know she would die in the winter? I honoured my promise to her.

Hundreds of motorcycles filled the church parking lot. Her sister-in-law even arranged for a motorcycle hearse. As the procession of bikes left the church, the clouds parted and the sun radiantly filled the sky. Nearing the graveyard, I noticed an eagle soaring the sky as if leading the ride. I felt an overwhelming sense of her presence.

The burial site was dug up in preparation of her awaiting casket. As I gazed at her coffin above the etched out hole in the ground, my body began to shake and tears flooded my bloodshot eyes. Suddenly I felt my kids on either side of me supporting my weakened body. I observed my elderly grandfather struggling to make his way to offer a rose on her coffin. I jumped to assist him. Jenny and I often accompanied my grandfather to church after our grandmother died. The loss of his granddaughter was taking a toll on him. As he placed the rose on her coffin, he said, "That should have been me." We wept in silent unison.

After the funeral service, everyone was invited back to my cousin's house. Her bike was mounted in the living room on display along with a shrine of pictures, trophies, and related memorabilia. It was breathtakingly beautiful and overwhelmingly surreal. I felt as though I was in a terrible nightmare from which I would awaken. This can't be real. Not?

The imprint of one's life does not manifest as the result of material wealth but rather the relational interactions throughout our journey. My cousin was a kind and gentle soul whose beauty impacted the hearts of many. An annual memorial ride evolved in her honour.

Although many questions remain unanswered surrounding the cause of her death, I have come to accept that she is not coming back. I choose to celebrate her life instead of harbouring tension and strife, asking questions to which we may never find answers. I choose to envision her riding free on the open roads in heavenly realms. Ride free, my beautiful sister, until we meet again.

The vanity of life on earth manifests in a variety of forms—striving for lifeless objects of no eternal value. Modern-day relationships are stifled through aimless distractions in the vortex of cyberspace and social media. War rages against the union of family and community. Death challenges the core of our very existence and paradoxically catapults us to embrace life in its spiritual construct.

I am not broken but rather under spiritual construction.

In late summer-early fall 2015, I received word from the college that they wanted to rollout the addiction worker program at a local campus. This news brought a great deal of relief and joy. I had been enduring extensive commutes to work for the past ten years. The potential opportunity to work close to home was an answer to prayer. My transfer was approved, and the program launch was well received in the region.

The transfer opened the opportunity for a new program instructor at my former campus. A good friend of thirty years had been enduring several trials and was in need of both a job and a place to live. He had an academic background in the field of addictions, so I made a recommendation to management on his behalf. He was afforded an opportunity to interview for the position and upon my recommendation was offered the job.

My daughter and I had started to come to terms with the realization that it may be time for us to live independent of each other. Our values about alcohol consumption in the home were in collision, and an increasing tension presented negative impacts concerning the tranquility of our home. We began to look for a new rental unit for her and my grandson.

After an exhaustive search, we finally found a beautiful two-bedroom apartment in the upstairs of a house. I agreed to gift her first and last month's rent toward her new venture. After helping her get moved and settled into her new place, I began renovations to my basement apartment to prepare it for rent. Several renovations were required, including new flooring, paint, and a bathroom door. My friend learned of my vacant apartment and proposed a rental deal. I accepted his proposal, and he moved in a few weeks later.

I owned my home for six years. That season in my life brought with it many trials and tribulations. I experienced sporadic cuts in income as well as increased household expenses and repairs. I endured suffering and loss due to broken relationships and death of multiple loved ones. In order to maintain the financial burdens, I endured years of sacrifice. I sacrificed my personal living space by renting rooms to recovering addicts. These sacrifices were necessary to supplement my personal income in order to afford the expenses necessary to maintain ownership of my home. My sacrifices also aided in overcoming a fear of being alone. I housed many recovering addicts throughout the six-year term—both short- and long-term stints. The recovery house experience brought with it many challenges and painful lessons about human behaviour and community building. The experience also afforded me an opportunity to glean a great deal of insight and wisdom on the core essentials of living in community and restoring healthy family systems.

The year 2016 brought with it a plethora of painful experiences. In May of 2016, I buried my grandfather, who was in his early nineties. My grandfather was a man rich in wisdom who emitted profound lessons from extensive lived experiences. He enlightened me concerning the topics of marriage, family, children, spirituality, biblical teachings, and the importance of embracing relationship encounters throughout life.

My grandfather and I spent a great deal of time together during the latter part of his life on earth. I spent many Sundays accompanying him to church, and he was well known as "Gramps" throughout my circle of friends. His roots were grounded in farming, and his elderly teachings reflected a love and wisdom for the land. Our heritage was of Native origin, so profound love and preservation of both the earth and his tribe (family) was deeply reflected in his storytelling. Gramps spent countless hours teaching me about the signs of the end of days, as woven throughout the Bible—especially as unveiled within the revelation of God written by John in the book of Revelation.

Gramps taught me about the essence of marriage as projected through his incessant expression of grief for my grandmother and his longing to go home to be with his deceased wife. From the moment my grandma took her last breath until I witnessed my grandfather release his last breath of life, he professed his everlasting love for her—an eternal love never to be separated by physical death.

I stood beside Gramps when Grandma took her last breath, and I held my grandfather's hand as he exhaled his last moment of life on earth. In the waking moments of my grandfather's remaining time on earth, I asked him if he was afraid to die. My grandfather's response took me by surprise. When Gramps professed he was afraid to die, I was startled and immediately asked him, "Why?" He explained that he was afraid to leave his loved ones behind. I watched in awe as a single tear gently trickled down his face.

As I held his hand, his grip tightened, indicating his intent to hold on until he passed over. In a soft-spoken tone, I encouraged Gramps to go home to meet Grandma in the light of our Lord. With those words, he inhaled a deep, peaceful breath of air and upon exhalation he drifted peacefully into eternal life. He was home at last, and his lessons remain forever embedded deep within my heart. I can still hear his heartfelt words echo, "I love you from the bottom of my heart."

As I reflect on the moments after witnessing my grandfather's last breath, I can visualize our hands connected and the sense of peace, warmth, and freedom in the atmosphere. A life well lived with no regret. A legacy birthed in the essence of family values and spiritual teachings.

As I write, I am in awe of the reality that death is not finite but rather infinite. Death is infinite in the eternal sense and in the essence of our loved one's imprint on the hearts of those remaining on earth. In many ways, death is not an end but a profound beginning if one awakens to the lessons.

Four months after my grandfather's death, my uncle passed away. The onslaught of pain continued for our family. My greatest struggle in dealing with the loss of my uncle was knowing that he died face down on the floor, alone in his apartment. This visual image unveiled a fear I came to face—that of dying alone. The gift my uncle left me was the opportunity to express this fear to my loved ones and to experience an unexplainable amount of gratitude for my recovery from addiction.

I am eternally grateful to experience life in sobriety and to live out my days walking in the destiny God has called me to embrace. I no longer have to fear dying alone because I am sober and surrounded by a loving family.

⬥

In July 2017, a call came that would announce a dreadful occurrence, one I had been silently anticipating for several years. While out for dinner, I received a call from my son. I recognized projections in his voice of terror, hysteria, and intense shock. He said, "Mom, Dad is dead!" As I hung up the phone, I became aware of my physiological state.

The day long anticipated had sadly arrived. I recognized an intrinsic state of shock manifesting. My hands were shaking, as was my voice. My heart rate was rapid, my face and neck were flushed, and I felt extremely disoriented and dizzy. We quickly left the restaurant after extending apologies for bailing on our food order. Fear captivated my heart at the thought of facing the reality that lay ahead. I could not grasp the idea of visualizing my son alone at the hospital beside his father's dead body.

The walk down the hospital corridor toward the emergency department was methodical as though we were cast in a heart-wrenching scene of a movie. Guided by staff, I paused at the door of Larry's hospital room. My heart pounded and tears streamed down my face as I captured the hysteria, pain, and shock on my son's face. He paced sporadically around his father's body as if lost in a maze. His body shook violently—captured in unbearable pain. Suddenly, he noticed my presence and we embraced. I was at a loss for words. What could I possibly say that would even remotely comfort my son in his desolation? All I could offer him in his moment of grief and sorrow was just to simply be present and support him through silent prayers of love and comfort.

The hospital staff was extremely supportive and compassionate, allowing the needed time to process the loss endured by the family. My son stepped out of the room momentarily to obtain a breath of fresh air and absorb the magnitude of his tragic experience. During his absence, I stood alone staring at Larry's body, as it lay lifeless before me.

I froze momentarily to comprehend the reality of my ex-husband's death. Larry had been my first love and husband for twelve years and the father of my children. Although our story had many dark components, in that moment, I chose to recall the light that emanated from the darkness.

I recalled a vision of Larry draped over our son's incubator after birth. The vision captured a father's pride and love for his newborn son. I remembered numerous occasions witnessing Larry passionately captivating an audience while gripping his microphone and resonating vocal excellence comparable to that of signed recording artists. Prominent managers expressed interest in Larry's vocal talent and awaited his original music. I captured the memories of our honeymoon cruise and the light that resonated from his face. The memories ran through my thoughts and heart as I looked upon a man who lost his family due to the inability to break free of his gripping addictions. As tears streamed down my face, I spoke soft cries of forgiveness and repentance. His story was left untold and seemingly unfinished at the young age of fifty-five.

Just then, the room began to fill with family members, and I was jolted back to reality as the tension in the room began to mount. I left the hospital room and joined my father in the hallway. My father had attended the hospital, at my request, to offer support to my son.

When my daughter arrived, I accompanied her into the hospital room and embraced her as she became overwhelmed with painful emotions. My son expressed needing to leave the hospital because he couldn't handle the extent of his emotional pain. My daughter wasn't long following her brother's lead.

I accompanied my daughter to a quiet room because she wanted to say goodbye to family members. Upon arrival at the quiet room, a family member uttered a painful comment that sent daggers piercing my heart. She said, "Larry's daughter is welcome to join us, but I don't want *you* in here."

I said, "I have no intention of coming in. My daughter simply wanted to say goodbye."

As we walked outside, I could barely catch my breath due to the onset of intense emotional pain, which had triggered a panic attack. Hurt triggered a rage response as I heard my daughter express her excruciating pain. She recalled the family's announcement that they had decided there would not be a funeral service for their father. A decision that was determined without the acknowledgement or input from Larry's children.

Upon returning home, I obsessively pondered the day's events. How could a family be so heartless as to deprive children the opportunity for closure? The kids never received closure while their dad was alive due to the entrenchment of his addiction. Now in his passing, they would be robbed of a crucial part of the grieving process.

Unable to contain my disdain towards the family's independent decision, I sent a few family members an emotionally charged message. I expressed my distaste for their heartless nature and total disregard of the children's desire to arrange a funeral service for their father. The message was rebutted around statements concerning funeral costs, which I confidently affirmed I would compensate. The following day I was informed by my son that the family had agreed to a private funeral service for the children on one condition—I was not permitted to attend.

The day of the funeral service arrived. My son went with his brother and aunt. My daughter hung out with me for support. After learning that my son had given her an incorrect start time for the service, my daughter experienced an acute panic attack and became emotionally unglued. I insisted on driving her and her boyfriend to the service and agreed to wait in the parking lot.

The service came to an end, and I saw my son walking toward my car. Suddenly, I heard my daughter screaming hysterically as she walked toward the car. I immediately felt my heart race uncontrollably and hopped out of the car, running toward her.

In a grief-stricken state, my daughter expressed her experience of the service. She explained that she observed my son struggling to leave his father's coffin so she proceeded to quietly inform him that I was waiting in the car if he needed me. Observing family members whispering amongst themselves, she began to feel uncomfortable. My daughter then told her boyfriend she wanted to leave because she didn't want to be around negative people. Suddenly she heard her aunt begin yelling profanities and calling her crude names. As my daughter walked toward the front door of the funeral home, her aunt tried to initiate a physical altercation. Her boyfriend interceded. My daughter continued walking away but began reciprocating through a verbal attack.

Upon hearing the news, I was devastated and enraged, so I joined my daughter in reciprocating a verbal attack. My son and my daughter's boyfriend interceded and directed us both safely to the car. Seeking every ounce of restraint, I slowly began driving away from the escalating shit show. I drove my daughter and her boyfriend back to my house and spent the evening offering her comfort and support. My son went with his brother to attend a family gathering.

The kids and I planned a celebration of life for their dad about a week after the funeral. It was an intimate gathering of friends and family in my daughter's backyard. They put together picture boards in his honour and had some of his vocal recordings playing in the background. We all pitched in for food to barbeque and enjoyed a time of fellowship outside in the warmth of the sunshine.

As I write of the closing events to Larry's life on earth, I am overcome, once again, with the effects of loss and grief on one's life. So many questions and reflections about life race through my mind. Often my reflections encompass present and future worries—longing for health, healing, wealth, and happiness in my children's lives.

Lately, however, I have found myself reflecting and dreaming about days past. I feel regret and pain stirring deep within as I ponder how I used to imagine my life would be. Most of the regret and pain I experience today is that of wishing I had more to offer my kids and regretting the many times I wasn't emotionally available for them because I was so consumed in healing from a history of trauma, abuse, and addiction. I also can fall prey to feeling like their lives could somehow be different if I had only done better by them.

Please forgive me. I want my children to know that some of the happiest days of my life have been watching their laughter and joy. The precious tiny moments that took my breath away

142

and filled my heart with joy. I want them to know that I am so deeply sorry they had to experience the loss of a parent at such a young age. I too can identify with that type of loss.

There are some things in life and through death that we may never fully understand. My saving grace has been learning to accept the things we cannot change, learning to live in each moment that God gives us, and learning to be grateful for the blessings bestowed upon us.

Chapter 6

The Joy Transition— The Beauty of Triumph

I hear the shofar bellow in the distant horizon, a cry to battle. The crossroads lay before me, and I ponder the atmospheric shift that comes with a choice in direction. Do I wander aimlessly amidst the status quo or take the road less travelled? Why do we fear the mysterious beauty of that which is unknown?

God does not give us a spirit of fear, yet I lack understanding of how to permanently break free of its gripping presence. God is all about giving us His power, love, and a sound mind. So how is it that my mind can become inundated with an onslaught of negative and confusing thoughts? God's ways and timing are often a mystery. There have been times in life when I have prayed, "God, if you don't want me here, then close the door, and if you do, then make a way even when the situation seems impossible." God often provides confirmation of His will by closing a door, but that doesn't mean that I like the feeling of uncertainty and loneliness.

God sometimes calls us to a place of "warring in rest." A time of transition and healing. A sacred place of deep fellowship with Him. Transition, like the change in seasons, presents the opportunity to shed the earth of disease and births healing and life renewed. As a seedling presses through the hardened earth, it springs forth a mesmerizing beauty. Transition exposes a period of pain and uncertainty, but perseverance produces maturity and triumphant beauty. Transition is not a representation of ending but of re-creating—of birthing new life.

Trauma had become my life's companion. Standing on the edge of the shoreline, I watched the distant force of trauma's roar locked beneath the ocean's depth. On the surface, the roar was diminished to that of the ebb and flow of gentle, soothing waves. The imprints in the ocean of time locked below a volcanic calm. Holding the key, I envisioned walking into the roaring depths of pain and sorrow. Unlocking the gate to my imprisonment, I stood firm as the battle raged around the core of my being. Letting go, I surrendered and rode the waves to freedom. Nature's force carried me to the surface, and I found rest in the sun's healing embrace. Devoid of the energy to fight, my body went limp to the rhythmic song of the water's dance.

The experience of joy represents unknown territory to trauma survivors. Choosing to embrace joy can create eustress—beneficial stress. When joy permeates the heart of a woman, it affects the beauty of the world. The joy of God is our strength that reaches down and pulls us out of incomprehensible evils. If we choose to hang on, God can transform us into the women He called us to be. We re-create our story to resonate with God's will. It is in the stillness that I heard His voice.

During my six year journey residing at my new home, I became aware of a hidden addiction—that of sex and love. This addiction manifested despite my intermittent relationship with James. This house was the first home I owned independently. First-time home ownership was an amazingly fulfilling experience but brought with it the realization of associated fear and loneliness.

The longing for companionship and love grew deeper with every passing day. Although I was surrounded by people, they were strangers who passed through the moments in time like that of a gust of wind igniting chords of vibration through a wind chime.

My kids and grandson also resided with me, but I still longed for the manifestation of childhood dreams. As a child, I envisioned a home filled with warmth, laughter, and love. A home that encompassed a happy family (uninterrupted by divorce, abuse, or addiction—mom, dad, children and a dog). After two failed marriages, riddled with abuse, addiction, and heartache, the longing for a loving, gentle husband seemed to be a hazy picture observed through the social media vortex. It certainly wasn't a clear portrait viewed on my mantelpiece.

Obsessed with filling this intrinsic void, I searched frantically through online dating sites for that one true love. The anticipation and search created a systemic rush of endorphins similar to that of obtaining my drug of choice. Preparation for each dating encounter created a euphoric high, which was inevitably followed by the crash of disappointment. Despite my continued disappointment, I chased the euphoria obtained through the onslaught of attention and would often schedule two or more coffee dates in one day.

I began to experience a great deal of agitation associated with the demoralization affiliated with this form of modern-day dating. The online dating vortex was riddled with pages of prospects to objectify, and it seemed to be a breeding ground for consumerism and sexual immorality. I began to grow weary of the shallow nature of such deceptive and meaningless connections. Unable to attain sustainable euphoria, I experienced an intrinsic wave of disgust and shut down all connection to online dating portals.

The week following my disconnect from online dating, I experienced a withdrawal-like state and sank into a depression. One day while out for a drive, I cried out to God in anguish. I said, "God, I have this unbearable ache, a sensation so elusive that it resonates my entire being. I maintain an intuitive sense that You have an amazing man of God for me—a man beyond my wildest dreams! God, if it is Your will that I remain single for the remainder of my days on earth, then *please* take this ache from me. And God, if it is Your will to connect me with a God-filled man, then could you please hurry it up?!" Within one month of crying out to God, I was to be connected to the man of my dreams.

I honestly believe that God has a sense of humour. Within a month, I would meet the love of my life. Dale and I connected through a mutual friend on Facebook. We both embraced a passion for riding motorcycles. Dale was riding with a group of sober riders, and I was searching for people in recovery who loved to ride.

The circle of friends that I rode with still engaged in drinking, and I was finding it difficult to maintain sobriety in an atmosphere of frequent intoxication. One day I decided to take a risk and reached out to Dale to inquire about the sober riding group. Dale's response involved sending me a link to a sober women's riding group. His response ignited a firecracker within me, and I gave him a firm piece of my mind. I challenged him to examine his ego and reflect on his knee-jerk reaction of recommending I ride with the girls. I also informed him that the majority of my riding companions have been males and that I am a skilled rider not to be judged as a novice because of gender.

I begin to laugh out loud as I recall our first interaction. I am experiencing a similar charge of intrinsic energy. I recall thinking, "What an egocentric, self-centred ass." In hindsight, I can see the glaring reflection of my own ego as I tantrum about the audacity of this man assuming I "ride like a girl."

I pause to embrace a warm fluttery feeling in my chest area—a feeling I embrace with deep fondness. As I view the words on my computer screen, I can see the outline of a beaming smile on my face as the sun illuminates the reflection on the screen.

Apparently, Dale was intrigued by my fiery personality, which stirred a curiosity to connect with this hot-headed biker chick *(still laughing out loud)*. Dale apologized for his biased demonstration of ignorance and invited me to join them on an outing to a swap meet. I was in the midst of building a new fence and informed him that unless it rained, I wouldn't be able to attend the swap meet. The weather forecast predicted sun and warm temperatures for the duration of the upcoming weekend. God, however, had other plans *(laughing out loud again)*.

On the morning of the swap meet, I awoke to the sound of rain on my bedroom window followed by an incoming text message on my phone. Dale was messaging to see if the rain was an indication I would be attending the swap meet and to inform me that his friends had cancelled so it would only be him and me in attendance. I agreed to hook up, despite the unexpected emotional experience of nervousness and excitement.

We decided to meet at a coffee shop on route to the swap meet. Pulling into the parking lot of the coffee shop, I parked my car and waited in anticipation. Thoughts raced through my mind. *Is this guy going to meet my expectations? I don't even know what he looks like. How will I recognize him? What if I don't feel comfortable? How will I get out of the commitment to accompany him to the swap meet? Why am I acting like this is a date? It is simply a connection to riding companionship.*

Suddenly, I see a vehicle pull into the parking lot that meets his description. As my heart started to race, I wondered why I felt so nervous. Looking into the side view mirror, I saw him for the first time. A smile of relief met my thoughts, "Oh, thank God, he is a nice-looking guy. I hope his insides match his outsides." As he began to approach my car door, I figured I should at least get out to meet him. Stepping out of the car, I told myself to calm down. At first glance, I was worried that we weren't the same height, but that fear proved erroneous. We grabbed a coffee and returned outside to engage in casual conversation. After conversing for about thirty minutes, I affirmed an intuitive sense that this guy was a safe companion for the day's events.

The first thing I noticed about Dale was that our communications were very natural and flowed with ease. We entertained a litany of topics during our commute to the swap meet. I felt a natural sense of ease and comfort in his presence. The connection I felt with Dale was pleasantly refreshing. We laughed, exchanged stories, and discovered many common interests. Arriving at the swap meet, we parked the car and Dale proceeded to open the car door for me. I was surprised to learn there are still a few gentlemen left in the world.

Having browsed the various vendor items at the swap meet, we non-verbally reciprocated a desire to spend more time together. We headed over to a lakefront restaurant to exchange further pleasantries over lunch. The atmosphere was breathtaking, and the company was surreal.

After lunch, I insisted we take a walk on the beach. I have always been captivated by the rhythmic force of the lake and enjoy the extensive sensory experience in its presence.

As I briskly walked to greet the water's edge, I embraced the childlike essence rising up within. Fully captured in the moment, I crouched down to grasp a handful of sand. I am entranced in the sensation of tiny granules of sand as they gently flow from my grip. I am reminded of a metaphoric description of surrender.

> We reach our hand into a massive body of water and try desperately to grab a handful of water to no avail. We cease trying to exert control over the fluidity of the substance. We surrender control and gently cup the fluid in our hand. At the point of surrender, we can experience nature's gentle embrace as we observe the water glistening in the palm of our hand.

As the final granule of sand departs from my grip, I returned to the reality of the moment. Standing to resume my visual experience, I was caught off guard. Unexpectedly, his lips met mine as though predestined in time. My face felt flushed and my body experienced sensations of being electrically charged. His lips were gentle and moist. Our lips flowed in sync with the gentle rhythm of the waves. The setting, the spontaneity, and the ambiance resembled that of a divine encounter. I was mesmerized in the natural beauty of the moment—a moment I will eternally cherish.

The magical essence of the first kiss is exhilaratingly magnificent. As our embrace released, I stood in awe of this man before me. I could see forever in his eyes. An intuitive "knowing" that this would be the first kiss of many more to come. A kiss that Dale claimed I initiated (*laughing out loud*). To this day, Dale and I engage in playful bantering about who initiated our first kiss.

During the next month, Dale and I spent countless hours together in an oxytocin-induced honeymoon state. We shared intimate details about our history, dreams, and aspirations. We experienced a mutual connection that is difficult to describe in words. At the centre of our connection was a reciprocated love for God. Without God at the core of our relationship, I don't think we would have endured the many trials that lingered in darkness.

Once again I find myself staring at the computer screen for countless hours trying desperately to find the words to complete the final chapter of this book. I ponder the reality that transitioning from a trauma-induced state to that of joy is troublesome and challenging. The ease at which I recall traumatic memories flows endlessly, yet piecing together the words to describe the beauty of experiencing healing is cumbersome. God, I cry out to You for the strength to persevere to the end. Lord, please download the final chapter and let it be a message of hope to all those suffering the devastating affects of trauma, grief, and loneliness.

Dale and I faced many challenges throughout our first month of dating. One of Dale's friends attempted to plant seeds of deception and stated his intention was to save me from future heartache. Dale's ex and her girlfriend also attempted to derail our relationship. A demeaning attempt to attack Dale's character was outlined in detailed text messages alleging an assault on his defects. I experienced a few friends presenting seeds of doubt and suspicion towards Dale's character and intention. Alluding to their possible motive of jealousy or pessimism, I struggled to maintain optimistic thoughts.

Also during this time I was in the midst of a court battle with Larry, which was distressing to say the least. The sober living environment also presented numerous challenges as we struggled to establish privacy amidst shared living accommodations.

Open and honest communication laid a solid foundation from which to endure the onslaught of attacks. We maintained our intimate spiritual connection despite the numerous trials that attempted to destroy our relationship.

Dale and I began to engage in conversations about marriage and started looking at engagement rings. Dale proposed to me while siting in the car underneath the Harley Davidson sign—a location I felt was ideal considering our passion for riding. We set a wedding date for June, exactly one month after our first kiss.

Both Dale and I had experienced two failed marriages prior to our union. Choosing to maintain an optimistic view of our past, we believed our experiences presented a great learning opportunity from which to grow.

We planned a very intimate, private, and simple celebration. Invitations went out to our maid of honour, best man, and their partners. The only others in attendance were my cousin's husband, who I chose to give me away, my girlfriend, who offered her photography services as a wedding gift, and the pastor and his wife.

A mutual passion for riding and the water resulted in the decision to ride to a beachfront restaurant located on the lake. Having an aversion to wearing dresses, I chose to wear white chaps and a white vest for my wedding attire. Dale and I made a decision to get tattoos as wedding bands, indicating a strong intention and commitment to an eternal union.

***

The wedding day had arrived, and we loaded up the bikes to set out on our journey. We had honoured God in a mutual decision to abstain from premarital sex. The anticipation was exhilarating both for our wedding and the consummation of our marriage. Having booked a room at a nearby motel, we packed our gear accordingly.

My girlfriend had blessed me with hair extensions as a wedding gift, and I had treated myself to a set of beautiful fake nails. Feeling an intrinsic sense of beauty, I suited up in my riding gear and was pleased with the reflection in the mirror. The best man and his wife rode with us to the lakeside destination. The sun was radiantly beaming amidst a cloudless sky. The weather was warm, and nature presented in full summer's beauty. The ride there was captivatingly beautiful, and I felt overwhelmed with joy.

Arriving at our destination, we joined our wedding party and headed toward the lake. The view was breathtaking: crisp blue skies surrounded with the gentle hypnotic rhythm of the lakeside waves. The sand was warm and beaming with crystal-like glimmers of the sun's radiant embrace. Massive rocks bordered the site, and the distant cawing of seagulls was nostalgic. As the ceremony was about to commence, my body shook with anticipation. The setting was picturesque as though taken from a tropical, romantic movie scene.

The pastor's voice interrupted my dream state and indicated we were ready to begin. Hanging on his every word, I was mesmerized by the purity and beauty of the matrimonial vows. Tears began to stream down my face due to an inability to contain the joy I felt in the moment—a moment that will remain etched in my memory for eternity.

The pastor presented us as husband and wife. Enveloped in each other's arms, we sealed the marriage vows with a kiss and joined our wedding party in shouts of joy and celebration. Our photographer captured the moments in time, and we all headed to the restaurant for the registrar signing and a celebratory feast. The ambience was breathtaking as if on a tropical island retreat. Finishing a delightful meal and time of fellowship, we headed out on the bikes to our honeymoon suite.

Dale carried me over the threshold of our room, signifying the beginning of our life together. The room was stunning— king-size bed, Jacuzzi tub, and a welcoming honeymoon basket of goodies. I felt my body glowing with anticipation of the night ahead. I came out of the bathroom to notice Dale had strategically placed our riding gear on the bed in a symbolic arrangement to that of union. Mutually embraced in a warm glowing sensation, we shared pleasantries about the ceremony.

As the sun began to set, we intuitively began to prepare for consummation. I headed to the bathroom to slip into my chosen lingerie despite an incredibly challenging experience attaching the garter belt to the stockings *(laughing out loud)*.

Emerging from the bathroom, I felt a tinge of nervous excitement. Dale's visual review of my appearance demonstrated a reciprocated excitement.

Our wedding consummation experience cannot be captured in words. I felt as though God had purified me to that of a virgin. In that moment, I fully understood the infinite wisdom and beauty in honouring God's word to abstain from sex until marriage. I experienced a stream of tears and a white light emanating from the marriage bed as we intimately embraced each other for the first time.

Our first sexual encounter was the most exhilarating and passionate experience surpassing all imagined possibilities. We embraced and connected passionately for hours, finally nodding off in the Jacuzzi tub from pure exhaustion.

The rising of the sun brought with it our first day as husband and wife. Still feeling the glow from our wedding day, I awoke and stared lovingly at my husband lying beside me. He opened his eyes and embraced me with a moist, love-filled kiss. Our mutual desire to remain captivated in the moment enticed us to remain enveloped in each other's arms for several hours.

Our stomachs began to grumble, and we decided to honour our bodies' indication to refuel. Loading up our bikes, we headed out to enjoy breakfast and a day of riding. We ended our day with a patio dinner at a restaurant located near a lakeside marina. Returning home at dusk, we snuggled into bed to recapture our first milestone celebration.

<hr />

Settling into the daily routines of life, the longing for privacy returned and initiated the search for a trailer. We obtained an amazing deal on a beautiful trailer in an upscale park—a welcomed retreat. The trailer was situated in close proximity to our jobs, which afforded us the opportunity to reside at the trailer for most of the summer months.

A serene setting that embraced nature was instrumental in the reduction of stress from our shared living accommodations at home. With fall approaching, we prepared to close the trailer for the winter and succumbed to the shared living accommodations as a temporary inconvenience. The following spring, we experienced extreme flooding on our trailer site and an onslaught of issues arising from the neighbouring residents. We decided to sell the trailer and were blessed to have made a profit. We invested the profit into another trailer at a park that offered a lake and younger residents. We enjoyed a season at this trailer park, but upon experiencing loud drunken neighbours, we decided to sell and establish a more sustainable solution for obtaining privacy at our home.

Dale had given notice to his landlord, and we slowly began to move his belongings into my home. A mutual desire to maintain equal contributions to our estate birthed a decision within Dale to pay off my debt; my contribution was the marital home. After attaining financial freedom through debt reduction, we began to contemplate the sale of our home. The continuing issues experienced through shared living accommodations with boarders, who were early in their recovery experience, fuelled this concept. Issues included chronic relapses, a lack of boundaries, disrespect, property damage, safety issues, extensive utility bills, and an increased atmosphere of stress and tension. These issues resulted in a chronic turnover of boarders, hence numerous strangers in our personal living space.

During the early years of our marriage, we also experienced several challenges to our health. I endured a litany of medical tests and doctor's visits concerning distressing symptoms relating to digestive and gastrointestinal issues. A few months prior to meeting Dale, I had my gallbladder removed and experienced post-surgical symptoms for about a year. These symptoms led to extensive research regarding nutrition, diet, and naturopathic remedies. Maintaining a holistic approach to health and wellbeing has finally resulted in healing.

Dale endured a steady decline in his spinal health and sought pain relief through holistic treatments such as chiropractic treatments and massage therapy as well as implementation of mind control. God uses all things for His good. As the result of experiencing personal health concerns, coupled with observing my mother's suffering due to chronic illness, I have become passionate about the study of holistic nutrition. I am currently pondering further education in holistic nutrition, which would allow me the opportunity to expand my capacity to support others in their healing journey.

As I write about our health challenges, I am recalling several reflections I have experienced regarding societal changes. Through extensive research and study of addiction, I have acquired personal views on sustainable solutions. As our society faces a national opiate crisis, it is becoming evident that change is needed.

All facets of study have led me to believe that recreating a healthy essence of community is of grave importance to future generations. One of my favourite sayings is, "It takes a village to raise a child."

I have witnessed a societal breakdown in family systems. In my experience, there are several contributing factors to this breakdown: an increase in divorce rates; soaring addiction-related issues; commercialism and debt; environmental issues and the effects on our food sources and natural resources; sexual immorality; increased isolation resulting from obsessive use of the internet, social media, cell phones, gaming, and other technological advances; and an overall disconnect in values gleaned from familial and cultural traditions—a lack of healthy community.

In my experience, I believe that the core essence of a healthy community must be rooted in constant contact with God and practical application of spiritual principles in all our affairs. I have worked very hard throughout my journey in recovery to "be the change I want to see in others." Although I have stumbled several times, hence resorting to default behaviours, I endorse myself for refusing to give up.

During the early years of our marriage, we also experienced several worrisome trials with our adult children. As our adult children tried to navigate the many societal challenges, they often made decisions and choices that posed potential risks to their finances, housing, health, stability, and family structure. On many occasions, I felt extremely powerless as I observed them struggling to find their way. Many nights I cried my self to sleep or became overwhelmed with fear and worry, which in turn created stress reactions that triggered an overbearing desire to want to run in and fix or control the situation. I learned to pause, pray, and allow God to direct my steps. He taught me when to support them, when to prayerfully give the situation to Him, and always to extend love. I began to recognize signs of unhealthy codependent patterns that I had created in our relationships. I became willing to learn to practice healthy loving detachment—and that was not an instantaneous or easy task!

⁓❧✗❧⁓

Four months into married life, Dale and I faced yet another challenge. In October 2016, I received notice from the college that I was going to be laid off. Fear gripped me at the thought of walking away from a ten-year career. Like a child, I had created, birthed, and developed the addictions program from its inception. I felt resentments brewing at the perceived injustice of being laid off without being offered the opportunity to continue in either my faculty head position or an instructor position at another campus. Their decision did, however, afford me a reasonable settlement package and entitled me to unemployment insurance. I decided to cease fighting and accept that if God had chosen to close this door, He would open another.

⁓❧✗❧⁓

During my time off, I began to feel God nudging me to return to ministry school. Initially I tried to ignore the nudges due to financial insecurities, but eventually I began to research various seminaries. Logically, I felt it made sense to attend a school closer to home, but my spiritual sense pulled me toward a ministry school in the United States. I had previously been enrolled there through correspondence but, due to time constraints, was placed on inactive status when I began designing the addiction curriculum. After a great deal of debate, I finally surrendered and applied.

Israel is a biblical name that means "wrestles with God." Through biblical studies and lived experience, I have learned that many people throughout history have wrestled with God.

There have been many times over the years when I have personally fought and wrestled with God. Each battle resulted in extreme self-criticism and internal chaos. I was greatly relieved when I learned that even people in biblical times wrestled with God. The ministry school epoch brought forth many occasions in which I wrestled with God.

In my experience, when God is "calling" me to pursue a directional change in life, it resembles an intuitive "knowing," like that of an incessant itch that will not dissipate until scratched. Ministry school was that itch calling me to a deeper relationship with my Creator. My only intention in obtaining a ministry degree was that of pursuing a more intimate relationship with God. As a gifted educator, I knew I would be more disciplined in my studies in a classroom setting.

I was accepted into the associates degree program. I attended a live, virtual classroom weekly with a small group of students from around the world. Our professor was a fireball known for her flamboyant hair colour. She was on fire for God, and her fire led to an outpouring of love and joy on her students. Throughout my studies, God continued to draw me into a deeper understanding of the revelatory wisdom gleaned through enduring suffering.

The Apostle Paul wrote the biblical book of Colossians while he was incarcerated in Rome. Near the end of the letter to the Colossians, Paul said, "Remember my chains." I found Paul's statement both challenging and encouraging. I imagined Paul handcuffed and chained in a dungy, damp prison cell struggling to write a letter. I embraced the perseverance and spiritual strength it must have taken to obey God's call on his life despite his gruelling circumstances.

As I continued my studies, I encountered scripture that encouraged readers to "rejoice in suffering." I began to pray about the pain and frustration I was experiencing as God repeatedly dealt with my resentment and resistance to experiencing suffering.

Throughout my life, I have built and lost several estates. I know what it feels like to access and rely on charitable non-profit organizations for food, financial assistance, and Christmas gifts for my children. I worked diligently throughout my life to build a home and future for my children.

As a single mother, I faced many challenges and would often escape to my prayer room to wrestle with God. One of the challenges of single parenting is the ability to adapt to multiple roles. During a verbal altercation with my son, he bluntly informed me that all he wanted was a nurturing mother. In that moment, I humbly realized how emotionally unavailable I had become. I was so driven to provide and obtain worldly possessions for my children that I lost sight of my role as a loving, nurturing mother.

I also realized that I had been trying to live vicariously through my children, giving them everything I wanted from my mother, and when they were unresponsive to my efforts, I felt a double rejection.

Today I realize that I could write a book about the numerous demonstrations of God's love and grace I have experienced during times of suffering and need. I find peace and encouragement in the verse that encourages us not to grow weary in doing good. Repeated exposure to God's explanation about suffering helped me break down resistance. I have learned that suffering builds strength, perseverance, and hope. Life will present challenges that can produce pain and suffering, but the faith-producing lesson is found in our reaction to each situation.

After I finished my associates degree, Dale and I began to weigh the pros and cons of selling the house. We were growing weary of sharing our personal living space, and although the added income was enticing, the associated stressors surpassed the benefits of financial gain.

The housing market was booming with predictions of an oncoming decline, so we decided to capitalize on the window of opportunity. We were continually drawn to a small country property on the outskirts of town, despite an intuitive sense cautioning against the purchase. We received a call from our realtor informing us that the owner of the country property had suddenly pulled her house off the market.

Discouragement began to set in due to feeling exhausted and frustrated as we observed the market declining and our window of opportunity closing. With one week remaining on our listing, we prayerfully decided to surrender both the housing search and outcome to God. At the point of surrender, our situation quickly began to shift.

We finally received an amazing offer with no conditions on the sale of our house, and we found the house of our dreams. We closed both deals with only days remaining on our listing. Once again, God did for us what we could not do for ourselves.

Moving day arrived, and as the house lay empty, I paused to reflect on a litany of memories racing through my thoughts. I visualized pushing my mother in her wheelchair as she captured every detail of my first home and smiled with pride. I felt a warm rush permeating my body as I envisioned my mother's glowing face looking down from heaven.

After settling into our new home, I decided to return to school. During my second year of university, I achieved a

Bachelor of Theology degree. Of notable mention was how I wrestled with God during my final thesis paper.

Our final thesis was a 5,000-word dissertation reflecting an in-depth study of the book of Revelation. In hindsight, I began to discern how a comprehensive understanding of suffering prepared me for the incomprehensible revelations of the end of days.

During my studies, I embarked upon a commentary that provided insight about the correlation to the soaring increase in addiction and evil during the end of days and the grave impacts on humanity. During the end of days, an extreme increase in pain and suffering will envelop mankind. In an attempt to resist extreme levels of pain and suffering, humans will seek refuge in highly toxic and addictive substances—addictions that will entrench mankind deeper into the wretched grips of unspeakable evils. My thesis attempted to unveil the love of God amidst the tragedies prophesied about in the tribulation.

As my thesis unfolded, I began to feel an urgency to share the love of God through practical demonstrations of His love, grace, and mercy.

Many people have asked me how a loving God could allow innocent people, especially children, to experience horrific trauma or tragic death. I don't profess to offer a comprehensive understanding, but what I do know is that God gave man free will. God wants us to come to Him of our own free will, to choose life over death, good over evil. I parallel this understanding to my relationship with my children. I want my children to love me and desire to be in relationship with me of their own free will.

If a person chooses to perform an act of murder, theft, or even rape, is that act their parent's responsibility? Can the parent control the adult child's action? Does the parent love the child any less? God loves me in spite of my sinful nature.

When I was healing from childhood trauma, I was very angry with God. I would scream, "Where were You when I was being abused and raped? Why didn't you stop the abuse? How could you allow such horrific acts of violence to happen to me?"

One day as I wrestled with God, I experienced a vision. God showed me where He was during my childhood trauma. I saw God above me in a transparent bubble. As I looked at Him in the bubble, I noticed He was weeping uncontrollably and seemed to be in a great deal of agony. His hand was extended out toward me in a desperate attempt to pull me out of my hellish circumstances, but the evils of my abuser's free will kept me out of reach.

If a child came home and told their parents they had been raped, would you blame the parent? The vision freed me from the pain and suffering of wondering why God didn't stop the abuse—it wasn't His fault.

I came to a place in my heart where I was able to forgive all of my abusers. I don't know what horrific circumstances occurred in their past that drove them to hurt others. Forgiveness doesn't dismiss their crime, nor does it mean I choose to befriend them; it simply means I choose to forgive so I am free!

As I ponder the magnificence of unveiling the love of God, the exquisite experience is that of a vast ocean's power as the waves ebb and flow to nature's call. A love that is boundless, eternal, and inseparable. A love worthy of surrendering one's life, even unto death. A love defined as *an intense feeling of deep affection* seems trite when remotely compared to the love of the God of the universe.

As I embarked on the study of the book of Revelation, I felt led to deeper study to unveil the love of God. While journeying through life, it is paramount to reflect on God's warning found at the centre of His Word: *"It is better to trust in the* LORD *than to put confidence in man"* (Psalm 118:8 NKJV). As life unfolds, it presents many trials and heartaches that can leave us feeling broken and alone. God in His abounding love and mercy promises never to leave nor abandon His children. God's commands and warnings are meant to be life giving and sustain us on the journey through life on earth. The world is full of seven-billion-plus pieces of God's heart, and as we get to know Him, we begin to absorb His affection for humanity. Our relationship with Him is the primary source and goal of revelation. The revelation that "God is love" is essential to the continuance of our life and gives us the endurance required to withstand trials and tribulation.

As I draw near to the end of my memoir, I am experiencing a battle raging in my thoughts. What current experiences do I include in my book? How do I articulate the ending? Are my readers being encouraged? Has the final chapter instilled a message of hope?

I stare out my window to observe the birds dancing in the air, the sun shining, and the wind gently vibrating through the trees. Spring is in the air and brings forth birthing of new life. Writing has birthed new life within me. I experience a sense of purging with each word I type. With only a few words remaining to be purged, I feel lightness in my body and a bounce in my step. Like a child running amidst nature's beauty, I feel a sensation of rebirth running through every cell in my body.

⁓⌀⁓

Completion of my degrees presented the opportunity to attend graduation ceremonies in the United States. Agreeing to attend graduation afforded me the gruelling task of dealing with extreme levels of fear and anxiety associated with travelling to another country. Soon after crossing the border, I experienced the onset of a panic attack and called Dale to help de-escalate my anxiety. Throughout the fourteen-hour trek to my destination, God helped me overcome a litany of fears.

The following day was filled with joy and excitement as I would meet fellow classmates for the first time since beginning our online educational experience. It was exhilarating to exchange God-filled memories of our two-year journey and to experience face-to-face fellowship. Our celebrations wrapped up with local sightseeing and feasting. During the drive home, I reflected on the celebratory events and felt a burning desire to travel arise in my spirit. I had an intuitive sense that the completion of my book would birth opportunities for travel.

⁓⌀⁓

The year following graduation brought forth a few stints of employment specific to frontline work in the field of addiction. The first opportunity was at a treatment centre two hours away from my hometown. The job was made feasible through on-site, overnight accommodations for staff. The compensation was commendable, and the employment role was very rewarding. Sadly, the position ended due to an unfortunate self-induced relapse of the owner of the facility.

The second employment opportunity consisted of an out-reach position at a local agency. For several months, I thoroughly enjoyed the role of supporting people suffering from issues resulting from substance use and mental illness. It was notably mentioned by my supervisor and colleagues that I excelled in the role. My position came to an abrupt halt when two individuals attending one of my process groups wrongly accused me. My termination experience was humiliating, unjust, and degrading. I was deeply distressed and saddened by the manner in which the situation was handled. I felt as though I had been persecuted for a crime I did not commit.

The final employment stint was a unique outreach worker role that involved rolling out a pilot project initiative. The role involved supporting street-entrenched populations in an outreach capacity and lending support to businesses in the city's downtown core. The pilot project's success attracted both media and political attention. In the midst of a national opiate crisis, the pilot project received rave reviews and was afforded continuance through sustainable funding sources. The position provided the unique opportunity for me to utilize prior experience as both an educator and addiction counsellor.

During the first few weeks on the job, I was to experience traumatic incidents with an individual on the street, which would gravely impact my ability to continue in the role. Numerous traumatic incidents eventually led to the individual being arrested and charged. The individual was released on recognizance and issued a no-contact order by the court for my protection.

Following release from jail, the individual breached the no-contact order in the presence of two witnesses, and to my dismay, the individual was not charged by police for breaching the court order. Upon further inquiry with police, I was informed that the incident was a "coincidental encounter." I also spoke with police about questioning the witnesses. The police officer's verbal explanation of questioning one of the witnesses was seemingly erroneous. The witness stated in writing that police never questioned them about the incident.

Several attempts were made to construct a safety plan that would allow me to continue my work on the street. Due to the imminent danger presented by the individual and circumstances unknown to me, a viable safety plan was not possible.

The toll of enduring six months of ongoing traumatic incidents had mounted. Upon learning that a feasible safety plan could not be implemented, I felt my ability to function in the presence of imminent danger had been depleted. I experienced indescribable levels of stress, fear, and anxiety. The ongoing chronic trauma had impacted my mental, emotional, physical, and spiritual wellbeing. I felt like I was in a constant state of "fight or flight."

I experienced repeated night terrors and bouts of insomnia. I would awaken in the middle of the night in a pool of sweat. Frequent checking of my house, yard, and car to ensure safety had become a daily ritual. I became easily startled and drawn to tears.

Feeling unable to cope with the ongoing situation, I decided to speak with my doctor about the grave impacts on my life. I was placed on medical leave effective immediately.

Currently, I am on a healing journey under my doctor's care. I am trying to stay focused on my health and overall wellbeing. Occasionally, distressing thoughts creep in about how the traumatic impacts are affecting my ability to return to a career to which I have dedicated twenty years of my life. The impact has been so severe that I face uncertainty about returning to work in the field of addiction.

The work-related trauma has also impacted my financial stability, family, relationships, and sense of security. Despite the feelings of grief and loss, I continue to surrender the situation to God and trust that He has a plan and purpose for my life.

Today gratitude has become a saving grace in my life. Today I choose to feel excited when waves of despair and suffering are lingering. God is with me in the valleys of life and often uses trials as a catalyst, launching me to new levels. I have used the medical leave as God's invitation to finish writing my book and purge the remaining fragments that were hindering my healing journey. Life today is full of demonstrations of God's healing power and unfailing grace.

As I start to write the final words of my memoir, I pause to articulate what my life is like today.

I am blessed with a newly renovated home acquired through hard work, sacrifice, and dedication. I share this tranquil environment with the love of my life. My husband, Dale, is an answer to prayer, a safe haven, and a gentle embrace during the storms of life. God has showered us with blessings of abundance, healing, and prosperity.

Through death, grief, and loss, I have acquired immeasurable lessons about living life to the fullest. I have overcome the grips of trauma, addiction, and abuse through the fragrant gift of forgiveness. God has taken me on a healing journey that has allowed me to recapture a connection to nature's beauty. A willingness to experience vulnerability has provided an opportunity to reconnect with an intrinsic childlike innocence and freedom.

A God-smack revelation about acceptance allowed me to see my children through God's eyes and in turn has created relationships built on unconditional love. I am proud of my children and amazed at their ability to flourish—especially when I get out of the way *(laughing out loud)*. Today I cherish and treasure beautiful moments spent with my children and grandchildren. The restoration of my family is an answer to countless prayers and a gift from God.

I patiently wait with excited anticipation of the career doors that God intends to open in His timing. I continue to maintain a deep "knowing" that the path will remain unknown until the completion of this book.

As I examine the nature of my life today, I can humbly confess that God has blessed me with a life beyond my wildest dreams.

Several years ago, someone asked, "If you had your life to live over, what would you change?"

I immediately responded, "Nothing! Every aspect of my life, up to and including this moment, has made me who I am today."

Writing has proven to be a very solitary endeavour and has given me the sensation of "coming home." Coming home is a metaphor for the re-creation of the woman God intended me to be.

I have realized that my purpose in life is simply to do the best that I can with each day that God gives me. I have learned to embrace the journey and resist the temptation to chase the destination. I have learned to memorize each step as it unfolds the magnificent story of God's plan for my life on earth. I have learned to embrace the opportunity to replace the old with new pathologies destined for joy-filled abundance and prosperity. I have learned to replace grumbling and pessimism with gratitude and acceptance.

The final chapter is not an end but rather a beginning, an invitation to venture into unknown territory. A childlike adventure, hand in hand with God.

I pray that everyone reading my memoir will embrace the call and join me in spreading a message of hope, faith, courage, and love.

My spiritual journey resonates a core message: *through God all things are possible*. I have overcome the many trials intended to take me out and have experienced the polarity of despair, which is *joy*.

May the love of God overwhelm you as you trudge the road of joy-filled destiny!

Bibliography

Alcoholics Anonymous (The Big Book). Copyright © 1939, 1955, 1976, 2001 by Alcoholics Anonymous World Services, Inc.

Booking and contact information:

Email: ashestobeauty019@gmail.com
Twitter: @AshestoBeauty19
Facebook: @memoirspiritualjourney

Ingram Content Group UK Ltd.
Milton Keynes UK
UKHW050641120323
418239UK00020B/1034

9 781460 011317